Letts

KS3
Success

Revision Guide

Mathematics
SATs

Levels 5-8

Fiona C. Mapp

Contents

Number

Algebra

Shape, space and measures

Handling data

Numbers

Factors

Factors are whole numbers that divide exactly into other numbers. For example, factors of 12 are:

1, 2, 3, 4, 6, 12.

Prime numbers

A **prime number** has only two factors, 1 and itself.
Prime numbers up to 20 are:

2, 3, 5, 7, 11, 13, 17, 19.

💡 *Note that 1 is not a prime number.*
Make sure you know the prime numbers up to 20.

Reciprocals

The **reciprocal** of a number $\frac{a}{x}$ is $\frac{x}{a}$

Example
The reciprocal of $\frac{2}{3}$ is $\frac{3}{2}$.

The reciprocal of 4 is $\frac{1}{4}$, since $4 = \frac{4}{1}$.

Prime factors

These are **factors** which are **prime**. Some numbers can be written as the **product** of their **prime factors**.

Example
The diagram shows the prime factors of 50.
- Divide 50 by its first prime factor 2.
- Divide 25 by its first prime factor 5.
- Keep on until the final number is prime.

As a product of its prime factors, 50 may be written as:

$$2 \times 5 \times 5 = 50$$

or
$$2 \times 5^2 = 50$$

in **index notation** (using **powers**).

💡 *When writing the prime factors of a number, remember to write the final answer as a multiplication.*

Highest Common Factor (HCF)
The **highest factor** that two numbers have in **common** is called the **HCF**.

Example
Find the HCF of 84 and 360.
Write the numbers as products of their prime factors.
$$84 = 2 \times 2 \times 3 \times 7$$
$$360 = 2 \times 2 \times 2 \times 3 \times 3 \times 5$$
Ring the common factors.
These give the HCF = $2 \times 2 \times 3 = 12$.

Lowest Common Multiple (LCM)
This is the **lowest** number that is a **multiple** of two numbers.

Example
Find the LCM of 6 and 8.
$$8 = 2 \times 2 \times 2$$
$$6 = 2 \times 3$$
8 and 6 have a common prime factor of 2, this is only counted once.
LCM of 6 and 8 is $2 \times 2 \times 2 \times 3 = 24$

Index notation

- An **index** is also known as a **power**.
  6^4 is read as **6 to the power 4**.
  It means $6 \times 6 \times 6 \times 6$.
  5^6 is read as **5 to the power 6**.
  It means $5 \times 5 \times 5 \times 5 \times 5 \times 5$.

  known as the base —a^b— known as the index or power

Powers on a calculator display
The value 5×10^6 means
$5 \times 10 \times 10 \times 10 \times 10 \times 10 \times 10$
$= 5\,000\,000$.
On a calculator display 5×10^6
would look like 5 06.
On a calculator display 7×10^{19}
would look like 7 19.

- The base is the value that has to be multiplied. The index indicates how many times.

Squares and cubes

- Raising any number to the **power 2** gives a **square number**. The original number is squared **for example**, $3^2 = 3 \times 3 = 9$
  Square numbers include:

1 — 1 x 1; 4 — 2 x 2; 9 — 3 x 3; 16 — 4 x 4

- Raising any number to the **power 3** gives a **cube number**. The original number is cubed **for example**, $4^3 = 4 \times 4 \times 4 = 64$
  Cube numbers include:

1 — 1 x 1 x 1; 8 — 2 x 2 x 2; 27 — 3 x 3 x 3

 Square and cube numbers can be represented by diagrams.

Square roots and cube roots

$\sqrt{}$ is the **square root** sign. Taking the square root is the **opposite of squaring**, for example, $\sqrt{36} = 6$ since $6 \times 6 = 36$.
$\sqrt[3]{}$ is the **cube root** sign. Taking the cube root is the **opposite of cubing**, for example, $\sqrt[3]{64} = 4$ since $4 \times 4 \times 4 = 64$.

QUICK TEST

1. 1 2 3 4 5 6 7 8 9 10 11 12
   From the above numbers write down:
   a any multiples of 3 b any prime numbers
   c factors of 20 d even numbers
   e numbers divisible by 5
2. Work these out without a calculator.
   a $\sqrt{100}$ b 8^2 c $\sqrt{64}$ d 2^3
3. Find the HCF and LCM of 20 and 25.

Positive & negative numbers

Directed numbers

- **Directed numbers** are numbers that may be **positive** (above zero) or **negative** (below zero).

Negative numbers Positive numbers

$$-8\ -7\ -6\ -5\ -4\ -3\ -2\ -1\ \ 0\ \ 1\ \ 2\ \ 3\ \ 4\ \ 5\ \ 6\ \ 7\ \ 8$$

- Negative numbers are commonly used to describe temperatures, for example, –5°C means 5 degrees below zero.

Examples –4 is smaller than 4   –2 is bigger than –5

Example Arrange these temperatures in order, lowest first: –6°C, 4°C, –10°C, 3°C, 2°C, –1°C.
Arranged in order: –10°C, –6°C, –1°C, 2°C, 3°C, 4°C

If you find working with directed numbers difficult, sketch a quick number line to help you. You need to remember the rules of multiplication and division. You will need to use these laws when multiplying out brackets in algebra.

Negative numbers on the calculator

The ⌷ +/– ⌷ or ⌷ (–) ⌷ key on the calculator gives a negative number.
For example, to get –2,
press ⌷ 2 ⌷ ⌷ +/– ⌷ or ⌷ (–) ⌷ ⌷ 2 ⌷
This represents the sign.

Example
$$-6 - (-3) = -3$$
may be keyed in the calculator like this; depending on your make of calculator.

⌷ 6 ⌷ ⌷ +/– ⌷ ⌷ – ⌷ ⌷ 3 ⌷ ⌷ +/– ⌷ ⌷ = ⌷
sign   operation   sign

Make sure you know how to key it into your calculator.

Multiplying and dividing directed numbers

- Multiply and divide the numbers as normal.
- Use these rules to find the sign for the answer:

Two **like** signs (both + or both –) give a **positive** result.
Two **unlike** signs (one + and the other –) give a **negative** result.

$(+) \times (+) = +$
$(-) \times (-) = +$
$(+) \times (-) = -$
$(-) \times (+) = -$
$(+) \div (+) = +$
$(-) \div (-) = +$
$(+) \div (-) = -$
$(-) \div (+) = -$

Examples
$$-6 \times (+4) = -24 \qquad -3 \times (-4) = 12 \qquad -24 \div (-2) = 12 \qquad 15 \div (-3) = -5$$

 Multiply or divide as normal, then put in the sign.

Adding and subtracting directed numbers

- When adding and subtracting directed numbers it is helpful to draw a number line.

Example

The temperature at 3 pm was 2°C; by 11 pm it had dropped by 7 degrees. What was the temperature at 11 pm?

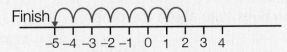

The temperature at 11 pm was –5°C.

Example Find the value of –2 – 7.   (Note the different uses of the minus sign).

$$-2 - 7$$

This represents the sign of the number, so start at –2.

This represents the operation of subtraction, so move 7 places to the left.

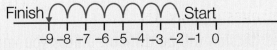

- When the number to be added (or subtracted) is negative, the normal direction of movement is reversed.

Example

$$-6 - (-1) \text{ is the same as } -6 + 1 = -5.$$

The negative changes the direction.   Move 1 place to the right.

- When two signs are combined then use these rules:

$+(+) = +$ } **Like** signs give
$-(-) = +$ } a **positive** result.

$+(-) = -$ } **Unlike** signs give
$-(+) = -$ } a **negative** result.

Examples

$-2 + (-3) = -2 - 3 = -5$ $-4 - (+4) = -4 - 4 = -8$

$5 - (-2) = 5 + 2 = 7$ $6 + (-2) = 6 - 2 = 4$

KEY TERMS

Make sure you understand these terms before moving on!
- directed number
- like
- negative
- negative number
- positive
- positive number
- unlike

QUICK TEST

1. The temperature inside the house is 12°C higher than it is outside.

   If the temperature outside is –5°C, what is the temperature inside?

2. Work out what the missing letters stand for.

   a $12 - A = -3$ b $-6 + 10 = B$

   c $-9 \times C = -36$ d $-8 - (D) = 2$

   e $120 \div (E) = -12$ f $14 + (F) = -6$

Working with numbers

Addition and subtraction

When **adding** and **subtracting** numbers, remember to align digits with the same **place values**, one above the other.

Example

4279 + 368

Line up the numbers first.

$$\begin{array}{r} 4279 \\ 368\ + \\ \hline 4647 \\ {\scriptstyle 1\ 1} \end{array}$$

Add the units, **then** the 10s and so on.

The one is carried here into the 10s column.

Example

2791 – 365

$$\begin{array}{r} {\scriptstyle 8\ 1} \\ 27\cancel{9}\cancel{1} \\ 365\ - \\ \hline 2426 \end{array}$$

Subtract the units column. 1 – 5 won't work. Borrow 10 from the next column. The 9 is replaced by 8 and the 1 by 11.

Multiplication and division

Questions on **multiplication** and **division** will be difficult unless you know your times tables.

Example

$$\begin{array}{r} 274 \\ 4\ \times \\ \hline 1096 \\ {\scriptstyle 2\ 1} \end{array}$$

Multiply the single-digit number by each digit of the large number.

Start with the units, then tens and so on.

When the answer is 10 or more carry the tens digit to the next column.

Example

$$403$$
$$3\overline{)1^1209}$$

Divide into the large number, one digit at a time.

Put the result of each division on the top.

Carry the remainder if the small number will not go in exactly.

Long division

A vase costs 74p. Tracey has £9.82. How many vases can Tracey buy? How much change will she have? Do not use a calculator.

$$\begin{array}{r} 13 \\ 74\overline{)982} \\ 74\ - \\ \hline 242 \\ 222\ - \\ \hline 20 \end{array}$$

Step 1: 74 goes into 98 once, put down 1.

Step 2: Place 74 below 98.

Step 3: Subtract 74 from 98.

Step 4: Bring down the 2.

Step 5: Divide 74 into 242, put down the 3.

Step 6: 74 × 3 = 222

Step 7: 242 – 222 = remainder 20

Tracey can buy 13 vases and has 20p left over.

Long multiplication

Example

A single plant costs 42p. Without using a calculator, work out the cost of 164 plants.

$$\begin{array}{r} 164 \\ 42\ \times \\ \hline 328 \\ 6560\ + \\ \hline 6888 \end{array}$$

Step 1: 164 × 2

Step 2: 164 × 40

Step 3: 328 + 6560

Cost = 6888p or £68.88.

💡 *Make sure your working is clear.*

Multiplication and division by 10, 100, 1000

To **multiply** by 10, 100, 1000 ..., move the digits one, two, three ..., places to the **left** and put in zeros if necessary.

Examples

15.2 × 10	= 152	Move the digits one place to the left.
53 × 10	= 530	Put in a zero, after moving digits one place to the left.
15.2 × 100	= 1520	Move the digits two places to the left.
53 × 100	= 5300	Put in two zeros, after moving digits two places to the left.
15.2 × 1000	= 15 200	Move the digits three places to the left.
53 × 1000	= 53 000	Put in three zeros, after moving digits three places to the left.

To **divide** by 10, 100, 1000 ..., move the digits one, two, three ..., places to the **right**.

Examples $15.8 ÷ 10 = 1.58$ $56 ÷ 100 = 0.56$ $18.2 ÷ 1000 = 0.0182$

When multiplying by multiples of 10 (20, 30, 700 ...) the same rules apply, except that you multiply the numbers first then move the digits to the left.

Examples $50 × 30 = 50 × 3 × 10 = 150 × 10 = 1500$
$2.4 × 20 = 2.4 × 2 × 10 = 4.8 × 10 = 48$

When dividing by multiples of 10 the same rules apply, except that you divide the numbers and then move the digits to the right.

Examples $6000 ÷ 20 = 6000 ÷ 2 ÷ 10 = 3000 ÷ 10 = 300$
$9.3 ÷ 30 = 9.3 ÷ 3 ÷ 10 = 3.1 ÷ 10 = 0.31$

Try to master all the different methods on this page as they are likely to be tested on the non-calculator paper and possibly the mental arithmetic paper too!

QUICK TEST

Answer the following questions.

1. a 279
      426 +
   b 639
      148 –
   c 276
       8 ×
   d 5) 1275

2. 279
   47 ×

3. 37) 925

4. Work out these without using a calculator:
   a 15.2 × 10   b 6.3 × 100
   c 21 × 1000   d 25.2 ÷ 100

5. A tin of soup costs 68p. Without using a calculator, work out the cost of 18 tins.

6. The cost of a trip is £10.25. If Mr Appleyard collects £133.25 how many people are going on the trip? Work out your answer without using a calculator.

KEY TERMS

Make sure you understand these terms before moving on!

- addition
- digit
- place value
- units
- subtraction
- multiplication
- division

9

Fractions

- A *fraction* is part of a whole. $\frac{2}{5}$ means 2 parts out of 5.

- The top number is the *numerator*, the bottom number is the *denominator*.

- A fraction such as $\frac{2}{5}$ is called a *proper fraction*.

- A fraction such as $\frac{12}{7}$ is called an *improper fraction*.

- A fraction such as $1\frac{4}{9}$ is called a *mixed number*.

If the numerator and the denominator are the same, then it is a whole one, i.e. $\frac{5}{5}$ = 1.

Addition and subtraction of fractions

The example shows the basic principles of adding and subtracting fractions.

Example

$\frac{1}{8} + \frac{3}{4}$ First make the denominators the same. $\frac{3}{4} = \frac{6}{8}$ (×2)

$\frac{1}{8} + \frac{6}{8}$ Replace $\frac{3}{4}$ with $\frac{6}{8}$ so that the denominators are now the same.

$= \frac{7}{8}$ Add the numerators. 1 + 6 = 7
     Do not add the denominators. The denominator stays the same number.

Example

$\frac{3}{4} - \frac{3}{16}$ First make the denominators the same. $\frac{3}{4} = \frac{12}{16}$ (×4)

     $\frac{3}{4}$ is equivalent to $\frac{12}{16}$.

$\frac{12}{16} - \frac{3}{16}$ Replace $\frac{3}{4}$ with $\frac{12}{16}$.

$= \frac{9}{16}$ Subtract the numerators. The denominator stays the same number.

Proportional changes with fractions

Fractions of a quantity
The word of means multiply.

Questions involving fractions are quite common on the non-calculator paper. Learn the quick way of finding a fraction of a quantity.

Example In a class of 40 students, $\frac{2}{5}$ of them are left-handed. How many are left-handed?

$\frac{2}{5}$ of 40 means $\frac{2}{5} \times 40 = 16$ students.

On the calculator key in: $\boxed{2} \boxed{÷} \boxed{5} \boxed{\times} \boxed{4} \boxed{0} \boxed{=}$

Alternatively divide 40 by 5 to find $\frac{1}{5}$, then multiply by 2 to find $\frac{2}{5}$.

Multiplication and division of fractions

When multiplying and dividing fractions, write out **whole** or mixed numbers as improper fractions. For example, rewrite $2\frac{1}{2}$ as $\frac{5}{2}$.

Example

$$\frac{4}{7} \times \frac{2}{11} = \frac{8}{77}$$

Multiply the numerators together.
Multiply the denominators together.

For division, change it into a multiplication by turning the second fraction upside down (taking the reciprocal), and multiply the fractions together.

Example
$$\frac{7}{9} \div \frac{12}{18}$$

Turn $\frac{12}{18}$ upside down and multiply with $\frac{7}{9}$.

$$\frac{7}{9} \times \frac{18}{12} = \frac{126}{108} = 1\frac{1}{6}$$

Give the answer as a mixed number.

The fraction key on the calculator

$\boxed{a^b/c}$ is the fraction key.

Example

$\frac{20}{30}$ is keyed in as $\boxed{2}\boxed{0}\boxed{a^b/c}\boxed{3}\boxed{0}$

This is displayed as

$\boxed{20 \ulcorner 30}$ or $\boxed{20 \lrcorner 30}$

The calculator will automatically cancel down fractions when the $\boxed{=}$ key is pressed. For example, $\frac{20}{30}$ becomes $\boxed{2\lrcorner3}$ or $\boxed{2\ulcorner3}$.

This means two-thirds

A display of $\boxed{1\lrcorner5\lrcorner7}$ means $1\frac{5}{7}$.

If you now press $\boxed{shift}\boxed{a^b/c}$, it converts to an improper fraction $\frac{12}{7}$.

Check: your calculator may have a $\boxed{2nd}\boxed{inv}$ instead of $\boxed{shift}$.

Equivalent fractions

- These are fractions that have the same value.

Example From the diagram it can be seen that $\frac{1}{2} = \frac{2}{4}$.

$\frac{1}{2}$

$\frac{2}{4}$

- A fraction can be changed into their **equivalent** by either **multiplying** or **dividing** the numerator and denominator by the same number.

Examples

$\times 3$

$\frac{7}{9} = \frac{?}{27}$ $\frac{7}{9} = \frac{21}{27}$ $\frac{35}{50} = \frac{7}{?}$ $\frac{35}{50} = \frac{7}{10}$

$\times 3$ $\div 5$

Multiply the top and bottom by 3.

Divide the top and bottom by 5.

Simplifying fractions

Fractions can be **simplified** if the numerator and the denominator have a common factor.

Example Simplify $\frac{12}{18}$.

6 is the highest common factor of 12 and 18. Divide the top and bottom numbers by 6.

$\div 6$

$\frac{12}{18} = \frac{2}{3}$ So $\frac{12}{18}$ is simplified to $\frac{2}{3}$.

$\div 6$

Make sure you understand these terms before moving on!

- denominator
- equivalent
- fraction
- improper fraction
- mixed number
- numerator
- proper fraction
- simplify
- whole
- of

QUICK TEST

① Work out the missing values.

a $\frac{7}{12} = \frac{14}{x}$ b $\frac{125}{500} = \frac{y}{100}$ c $\frac{19}{38} = \frac{76}{z}$

② Work out the following:

a $\frac{2}{9} + \frac{3}{27}$ b $\frac{3}{5} - \frac{1}{4}$ c $\frac{6}{9} \times \frac{72}{104}$ d $\frac{8}{9} \div \frac{2}{3}$

③ $\frac{5}{8}$ of a class of 24 pupils walk to school. How many pupils walk to school?

Decimals

What are decimals?

- A **decimal point** separates whole-number columns from fractional columns.

Example

Thousands	Hundreds	Tens	Units		Tenths	Hundredths	Thousandths
6	7	1	4	•	2	3	8

Decimal point

The 2 means $\frac{2}{10}$. The 3 means $\frac{3}{100}$. The 8 means $\frac{8}{1000}$.

Recurring decimals

- A decimal that **recurs** is shown by placing dots over the first and last digits in the group that is repeated.

Example $0.66666\ldots$ $= 0.\dot{6}$ Place a dot over the 6.

$0.147147\ldots$ $= 0.\dot{1}4\dot{7}$ Place dots over the 1 and the 7.

 Remember, hundredths are smaller than tenths, $\frac{3}{100}$ is smaller than $\frac{2}{10}$.

Decimal places (dp)

When rounding to a specified number of **decimal places**:

- Look at the digit in the last 'required' place. Rounding 8.347 to 2 dp look at the 4 in the second decimal place.
- Look at the number after it which is not needed, in this case the 7.
- If it is **5 or more** round up the last digit (7 is greater than 5, so round the 4 up to a 5).
- If it is **less than 5**, the digit remains the **same**.
- 8.347 = 8.35 (to 2 dp).

Examples

16.59 = 16.6 to 1 dp

8.435 = 8.44 to 2 dp

12.34 = 12.3 to 1 dp

Multiplying and dividing by numbers between 0 and 1

- When **multiplying** by numbers between 0 and 1, the result is **smaller** than the starting value.
- When **dividing** by numbers between 0 and 1, the result is **bigger** than the starting value.

Examples

4 × 0.1 = 0.4	4 ÷ 0.1 = 40
4 × 0.01 = 0.04	4 ÷ 0.01 = 400
4 × 0.001 = 0.004	4 ÷ 0.001 = 4000

The result is **smaller** than the starting value.

The result is **bigger** than the starting value.

 Questions involving multiplication and division by numbers between 0 and 1 are common on the non-calculator paper and the taped mental arithmetic test. To practise, set yourself a short test and check your answers with a calculator.

Ordering decimals

When ordering decimals:

- First write them all with the same number of digits after the decimal point.
- Then compare whole numbers, digits in the tenths place, digits in the hundredths place, and so on.

Example

Arrange these numbers in order of size, smallest first: 4.27, 4.041, 4.7, 6.4, 2.19, 4.72.

First rewrite them: 4.270, 4.041, 4.700, 6.400, 2.190, 4.720

Then reorder them: 2.190   4.041   4.270   4.700   4.720   6.400

Have a quick check that all values are included.   The zero is worth less than than the 2.

Calculations with decimals

Calculations with decimals are similar to calculating with whole numbers.

Examples

1 Add 6.21 and 4.9

```
  6.21
  4.90 +
 11.11
    1
```

Align the decimal points.

This is the same as 4.9.

The decimal points in the answer will be in line.

3 Multiply 12.3 by 7

```
 12.3
    7 ×
  861
   1 2
```
Answer = 86.1

$123 \times 7 = 861$, ignoring the decimal point. Since 12.3 has one number after the decimal point then so must the answer.

2 Subtract 6.2 from 12.81.

```
 12.81
  6.20 −
  6.61
```

4 Divide 25.8 by 6.

```
     4.3
 6 )25.⁸8
```

Divide as normal, placing the decimal points in line.

When adding or subtracting decimals make sure they have the same number of decimal places, e.g. 4.9 = 4.90.

KEY TERMS

Make sure you understand these terms before moving on!

- decimal place
- decimal point
- recurring

QUICK TEST

Work out the answers to the following questions.

1
- a 27.9
  143.07 +
- b 16.05
  12.21 −
- c 27.8
  3 ×
- d 4)62.8

2
- a 60 × 30
- b 6 × 30
- c 0.6 × 30
- d 150 ÷ 5
- e 150 ÷ 0.5
- f 250 ÷ 0.005

3 Arrange these numbers in order of size, smallest first.
- a 0.62, 0.03, 0.84, 0.037
- b 27.06, 22.53, 22.507, 27.064

4 Round these numbers to 2 decimal places.
- a 12.736
- b 9.255
- c 4.172

Percentages 1

- *Percentages* are fractions with a denominator of 100.
- % is the percentage sign.
- 75 per cent means $\frac{75}{100}$ (this is equal to $\frac{3}{4}$).

Percentages of a quantity

Example

Find 15% of £650.

Replace the word 'of' with a × sign.

Rewrite the percentage as a fraction.

$\frac{15}{100} \times 650 = £97.50$

On the calculator key in:

| 1 | 5 | ÷ | 1 | 0 | 0 | × | 6 | 5 | 0 | = |

- To work this out mentally, find:
  10% = 650 ÷ 10 = £65
  5% is half of £65 = £32.50
  Add the two together to give £97.50.

Example

Work out $17\frac{1}{2}$ % of 360 without a calculator.

$$10\% \ \text{of} \ 360 = 36$$
$$5\% \ \text{of} \ 360 = 18$$
$$2\tfrac{1}{2}\% \ \text{of} \ 360 = \ 9$$

So $17\frac{1}{2}$% of 360 = 36 + 18 + 9
= 63

Percentage questions appear frequently at KS3. If there is a percentage question on the non-calculator paper, work out 10% as shown in the examples.

One quantity as a percentage of another

Rule: To make a fraction into a **percentage**, **multiply** by 100%.

Make a fraction with the two numbers. Multiply by 100% to get a percentage.

Example

A survey shows that 26 people out of 45 preferred 'Supersuds' washing powder. What percentage preferred Supersuds?

$\frac{26}{45} \times 100\% = 57.\dot{7}\% = 57.8\%$ (1 dp)

On the calculator key in | 2 | 6 | ÷ | 4 | 5 | × | 1 | 0 | 0 | = |

Example

In a carton of milk, 6.2 g of the contents are fat. If 2.5 g of the fat is saturated what percentage of the fat is this?

Make the fraction. $\frac{2.5}{6.2} \times 100\% = 40.3\%$ (1 d.p.)
× by 100%

Increasing and decreasing by a percentage

Percentages often appear in real-life problems.
You may need to find the new value when an amount
has been **increased** or **decreased** by a percentage.

Example

A new car was bought for £8600. After 2 years, it had lost 30% of its value.
Work out the value of the car after 2 years, using a non-calculator method.

100% = £8600

10% = 8600 ÷ 10
= £860

30% = 860 × 3
= £2580

To find 10% remember
to divide by 10.
Remember 'of' means
multiply (×).

This is the same as multiplying
by $1 - \frac{30}{100} = \frac{70}{100}$ or 0.7.
8600 × 0.7 = £6020
This is a little more difficult
without a calculator.

Value of car after 2 years = original – decrease
= 8600 – 2580 = £6020

Example

In 1998 the average price of a 3-bedroomed house was £72 000.
By 2001, the average price of a 3-bedroomed house had risen by 27%.
Work out the average price in 2001.

100% = £72 000

Percentage increase = 27% of £72 000

$= \frac{27}{100} \times 72\,000 = £19\,440$

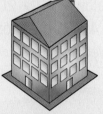

Remember to answer the whole question!

Average price of house in 2001 = £72 000 + £19 440 = £91 440

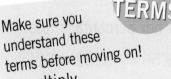
QUICK TEST

1. Out of the 30 people at a bus stop, 10% wear glasses. How many people wear glasses?
2. 25% of the students in year 9 choose Maths as their favourite subject. If there are 140 students in the year, how many choose Maths?
3. If 20% of a number is 8, what is the number?
4. Of the 62 cars in a car park, 14 are white. What percentage are white? **c**
5. The top mark in a Maths test was 59 out of 72. Write this as a percentage. **c**
6. A jumper costs £60. If its price is reduced by 15% in a sale, how much does it now cost?
7. The number of people who go swimming in the morning is 30. If this rises by 20%, how many now go swimming in the morning?

Percentages 2

Repeated percentage change

Example A clothes shop has a sale. For each day of the sale, prices are reduced by 20 per cent of the prices on the day before. A jumper has a price of £45 on Monday. If the sale starts on Tuesday, how much does Mary pay for the jumper if she buys it on Wednesday?

Monday price = £45

Tuesday reduction = $\frac{20}{100}$ × 45 = £9

New price = £45 – £9 = £36

Wednesday reduction
    = $\frac{20}{100}$ × 36 = £7.20

New price = £36 – £7.20
        = £28.80

Do not just calculate 2 × 20 = 40% reduction over two days.

Mary paid £28.80.

Example

A car was bought in 1999 for £10 500. Each year the car depreciates (goes down) in value by 8%. How much is the car worth after three years?

1999 £10 500

2000 $\frac{8}{100}$ × £10 500 = £840

New value = 10 500 – 840 = £9660

2001 $\frac{8}{100}$ × 9660 = £772.80

New value = 9660 – 772.80 = £8887.20

2002 $\frac{8}{100}$ × 8887.20 = £710.98
                            (nearest penny)

The car is worth 8887.20 – 710.98
            = £8176.22

> *Show your working clearly. Always work these problems out step by step.*

Profit and loss

- If you buy an article, the price you pay is the **cost price**.
- If you sell the article, the price you sell it for is the **selling price**.
- **Profit** (or **loss**) is the difference between the cost price and the selling price.

You can write the profit or loss as a **percentage** of the original price.

Percentage profit
    = $\frac{\text{profit}}{\text{original price}}$ × 100%

Percentage loss
    = $\frac{\text{loss}}{\text{original price}}$ × 100%

Example A shop bought a television for £350. A customer later bought the television for £680. Find the percentage profit.

Profit = £680 – £350 = £330

% profit = $\frac{\text{profit}}{\text{original price}}$ × 100%
        = $\frac{330}{350}$ × 100%
        = 94% profit

Example Jacqueline bought a sofa for £569, but later sold it for £352.
Calculate her percentage loss.

Loss = £569 – £352 = £217

Percentage loss = $\frac{217}{569}$ × 100%
                = 38.1% loss

> *When answering questions that involve profit and loss, remember to multiply by 100% and divide by the original or cost price.*

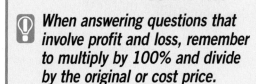

Taxation

- **Value added tax** (VAT) is the amount added to bills for services and purchases.
- Currently VAT is $17\frac{1}{2}\%$.

Example
The price of a computer is £1150 plus VAT at $17\frac{1}{2}\%$.
Work out the final cost inclusive of VAT.
VAT: 17.5% of £1150

$\frac{17.5}{100} \times £1150 = £201.25$

This can be calculated by multiplying by $1 + \frac{17.5}{100} = 1.175$.

Then 1.175 is known as the **multiplier**.

Total cost = £1150 + £201.25 = £1351.25
These are 'percentages of' questions again!

Reverse percentage problems (Level 8)

In reverse percentage problems you calculate the original quantity from the changed quantity.

Example The price of a television is reduced by 20% in the sales.
It now costs £250. What was the original price?
- The sale price is 100% − 20% = 80% of the pre-sale price.

$\frac{80}{100} = 0.8$

$0.8 \times (\text{price}) = £250$

$\text{price} = \frac{250}{0.8} = £312.50$

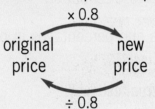

You need to find 80% of the original price, not 80% of the new one.

 Always check the answer is sensible.
Is the original price more than the sale price?

KEY TERMS

Make sure you understand these terms before moving on!
- cost price
- loss
- multiplier
- percentage
- percentage loss
- percentage profit
- profit
- selling price
- value-added tax

QUICK TEST

1. A house was bought for £65 000. Each year it rose in value by 10%. How much is the house worth three years later? **c**

2. Work out the percentage profit or loss on these items: **c**

   a cost price £120, selling price £75

   b cost price £204, selling price £263

   c cost price £144, selling price £128

3. VAT is added to a telephone bill of £72.40. Find the total amount to be paid. **c**

4. (Level 8) The price of a hi-fi system is reduced by 15% in the sales. It now costs £350. What was the original price? **c**

Equivalents

Useful equivalents

Fractions, **decimals** and **percentages** all refer to the same number but are just written in different ways.

The table shows:
- some common fractions and their **equivalents**, which you need to learn
- how to convert

$$\text{fractions} \xrightarrow{\text{to}} \text{decimals} \xrightarrow{\text{to}} \text{percentages.}$$

Fraction	Decimal	Percentage
$\frac{1}{2}$ $\xrightarrow{1 \div 2}$	0.5 $\xrightarrow{\times 100\%}$	50%
$\frac{1}{3}$	$0.\dot{3}$	$33.\dot{3}\%$
$\frac{2}{3}$	$0.\dot{6}$	$66.\dot{6}\%$
$\frac{1}{4}$	0.25	25%
$\frac{3}{4}$	0.75	75%
$\frac{1}{5}$	0.2	20%
$\frac{1}{8}$	0.125	12.5%
$\frac{3}{8}$	0.375	37.5%
$\frac{1}{10}$	0.1	10%
$\frac{1}{100}$	0.01	1%

Ordering different numbers

When putting fractions, decimals and percentages in order of size, it is best to change them all to **decimals** first.

Example Place in order of size, smallest first:
$\frac{1}{4}$, 0.241, 29%, 64%, $\frac{1}{3}$

0.25, 0.241, 0.29, 0.64, $0.\dot{3}$ Put into decimals first.

0.241, 0.25, 0.29, $0.\dot{3}$, 0.64   Now order.

0.241, $\frac{1}{4}$, 29%, $\frac{1}{3}$, 64%   Now rewrite in their original form.

> *Make sure you put the values in the order the question says. Ask a friend to test you on common equivalent fractions, decimals and percentages.*

1. Complete the table.

2. Arrange these numbers in order of size, smallest first:
   $\frac{2}{3}$, 0.25, $\frac{5}{9}$, 84%, $\frac{9}{10}$.

Fraction (simplest form)	Decimal	Percentage
		75%
$\frac{2}{5}$		
	$0.\dot{3}$	
	0.6	
		20%

KEY TERMS

Make sure you understand these terms before moving on!
- decimal
- equivalent
- fraction
- percentage
- BIDMAS
- positive
- negative

Using a calculator

Order of operations

Bidmas is a made-up word that helps you to remember the order in which to do calculations.

B I D M A S

Brackets Indices Division Multiplication Addition Subtraction

This just means that brackets are carried out first, then the other operations are done in order.

Examples $(2 + 4) \times 3 = 18$ $6 + 2 \times 4 = 14$ Not 32 because multiplication is done first.

💡 *It is very important that you can use your own calculator.*
Practise questions with a friend so that you become confident.

Important Calculator Keys

Make sure you can use your calculator.

shift or 2nd or Inv allow 2nd functions to be carried out.

– or +/– changes **positive** numbers to **negative** ones.

bracket keys

Often puts the ×10 part in when working in standard form.

Pressing shift EXP often gives π.

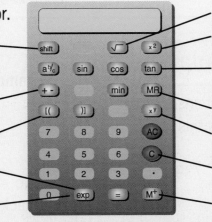

square root

square button

trigonometric buttons

memory keys

Works out powers.

Cancels only the last key you pressed.

memory keys

This calculator is made up just to show you some of the important calculator keys.

Example $\frac{15 \times 10 + 46}{9.3 \times 2.1}$ = 10.04 (2 dp) This may be keyed in as:

[(1 5 × 1 0 + 4 6)} ÷ [(... 9 . 3 × 2 . 1)} =

Now try using the memory keys. Write down the key sequence for your calculator.

Calculating powers

y^x or x^y is used for calculating powers such as 2^7.

- Use the power key on the calculator to work out 2^7.
- Write down the calculator keys used.
- Check you obtain the answer 128.

QUICK TEST

① Work these out on your calculator. Ⓒ

a $\frac{6.2 + (4.6)^2}{\sqrt{3.2 \times 1.7}}$ b $\frac{\sqrt{9.4 - 2.7}}{6.1 + 8.2}$

b $\frac{27.1 \times 6.4}{9.3 + 2.7}$ b $\frac{(9.3)^4}{2.7 \times 3.6}$

② Jonathan's calculator display shows
1.52 06.
Write down what the display means.

Checking calculations

Calculations

When solving problems you should round the answers sensibly.

Example
95.26 × 6.39 = 608.7114 = 608.71
(2 dp)
Round to 2 dp because the values in the question are to 2 dp.

💡 *You will lose marks if you do not write money to 2 dp If the answer to a money calculation is £9.7, you must write it to 2 dp as £9.70.*

Example
Paint is sold in 8-litre tins. Sandra needs 27 litres of paint. How many tins must she buy?

27 ÷ 8 = 3 remainder 3
Sandra needs four tins of paint.
Sandra would not have enough paint with three tins, since she would be three litres short. Hence the number of tins of paint must be rounded up.
When rounding remainders, consider the context of the question.

Checking calculations

When checking calculations, you can reverse the process like this.

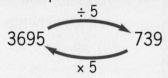

3695 ÷ 5 → 739
3695 ← ×5 739

Example

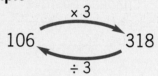

106 ×3 → 318
106 ← ÷3 318

106 × 3 = 318
Check: 318 ÷ 3 = 106

Significant figures (sf or sig fig)

Apply the same rule as with decimal places: if the next digit is 5 or more, round up. The first **significant figure** is the first digit that is not zero. The second, third, fourth,... significant figures follow on after the first digit. They may or may not be zeros.

Examples

6.4027 has 5 sf
1st 2nd 3rd 4th 5th

0.0004701 has 4 sf
1st 2nd 3rd 4th

Examples

Number	to 3 sf	to 2 sf	to 1 sf
4.207	4.21	4.2	4
4379	4380	4400	4000
0.006 209	0.006 21	0.0062	0.006

When rounding, take care that you do not leave off digits that you need.

💡 *After rounding the last digit you must fill in the end zeros, e.g. 4380 = 4400 to 2 sf (not 44).*

Estimates and approximations

Estimating is a good way of checking answers.

- Round the numbers to 'easy' numbers, usually to the nearest 10, 100 or 1000.
- Use these easy numbers to work out the **estimate**.
- Use the symbol ≈, which means '**approximately equal to**'.

When multiplying or dividing, never **approximate** a number with zero.
Use 0.1, 0.01, 0.001, …

Examples

a $12 \times 406 \approx 10 \times 400 = 4000$

b $(6.29)^2 \approx 6^2 = 36$

c $\frac{296 \times 52.1}{9.72 \times 1.14} \approx \frac{300 \times 50}{10 \times 1} = \frac{15000}{10} = 1500$

d $0.096 \times 79.2 \approx 0.1 \times 80 = 8$

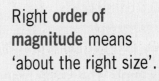 *Questions that involve approximating are likely to be on the non-calculator paper. For most of these questions, you are expected to round to 1 sf. Even if you find the calculations difficult, show your approximations to pick up marks for method.*

Example

Q Jack works out $\frac{9.6 \times 103}{(2.9)^2}$.

a Estimate the answer to this calculation, without using a calculator.

b Jack's answer is 1175.7. Is this the right order of magnitude?

A **a** Estimate $\frac{9.6 \times 103}{(2.9)^2} \approx \frac{10 \times 100}{3^2} = \frac{1000}{9} \approx \frac{1000}{10} = 100$

Right **order of magnitude** means 'about the right size'.

b Jack's answer is not the right order of magnitude. It is 10 times too big.

Examples

$109.6 + 0.0002 \approx 110 + 0 = 110$ $63.87 - 0.01 \approx 64 - 0 = 64$

When adding and subtracting, very small numbers may be approximated to zero.

 KEY TERMS

Make sure you understand these terms before moving on!
- approximate
- approximately equal to
- estimate
- order of magnitude
- significant figure

QUICK TEST

1 Round the following numbers to 3 significant figures (3 sf).
a 0.003 786   b 27 490   c 307 250

2 Estimate the answer to $\frac{(29.4)^2 + 106}{2.2 \times 5.1}$.

3 Sukhvinder decided to decorate her living room. The total area of the walls was 48 m². If one roll of wallpaper covers 5 m² of wall, how many rolls of wallpaper will Sukvhinder need?

4 Thomas earned £109.25 for working a 23-hour week. How much did he earn per hour? Estimate, then use a calculator.

Ratio

What is a ratio?

A **ratio** is used to compare two or more quantities. The symbol for '**Compared to**' is **two dots**(:). For example, '16 boys compared to 20 girls' can be written as 16 : 20.

To **simplify** ratios, divide both parts of the ratio by the highest common factor.

For example, 16 : 20 = 4 : 5 (divide both parts by 4).

Examples

Simplify the ratio 21:28.

21 : 28 = 3 : 4 (Divide both parts by 7.)

The ratio of yellow flowers to blue flowers can be written as:

$$10 : 4 = \frac{10}{2} : \frac{4}{2}$$
$$= 5 : 2$$

In other words, for every 5 yellow flowers there are 2 blue flowers.

To express the ratio 5 : 2 in the ratio n : 1 divide both sides by 2.

$$5 : 2 = \frac{5}{2} : \frac{2}{2} = 2.5 : 1$$

Best buys

You can compare unit amounts to decide which is the better value for money.

£2.81   750 g

Example The same brand of breakfast cereal is sold in two different-sized packets. Which packet represents the better value for money?

- Find the cost per gram for each packet.

125 g cost £1.06   Cost of 1 g = 106 ÷ 125 = 0.848p.
750 g cost £2.81   Cost of 1 g = 281 ÷ 750 = 0.3746p.

£1.06

- Since the 750 g packet costs less per gram, it is the better value for money.

Sharing a quantity in a given ratio

- Add up the total parts.
- Work out what one part is worth.
- Work out what the other parts are worth.

Example

A forest covers 25 000 hectares. Oak and ash trees are planted in the forest in the ratio 2 : 3. How many hectares do the ash trees cover?

- 2 + 3 = 5 parts
- 5 parts = 25 000 hectares
- 1 part = $\frac{25\,000}{5}$ = 5000 hectares

Ash has 3 parts. So 3 × 5000 = 15 000 hectares.

As a quick check, work out the number of hectares the oak trees cover. The total of the oak and ash should be equal to 25 000 hectares.

Increasing and decreasing in a given ratio

- Divide to get one part
- Multiply for each new part

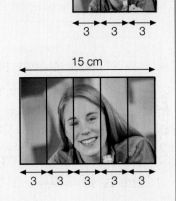

9 cm

3 3 3

15 cm

3 3 3 3 3

Example
A photograph of length 9 cm is to be enlarged in the ratio
5 : 3. What is the length of the **enlarged** photograph?
- Divide 9 cm by 3 to find the size of one part or share.
  9 ÷ 3 = 3 cm
- Now multiply this by 5.
  5 × 3 = 15 cm is the length of the enlarged photograph.

Example
It took 8 people 6 days
to build a house. At the
same rate how long
would it take 3 people?

- Time for 8 people = 6 days.
- Time for 1 person = 8 × 6 = 48 days.
It takes one person longer to build the
house.
- Time for 3 people = $\frac{48}{3}$ = 16 days.

3 people will take $\frac{1}{3}$ of the time taken by
1 person.

Example
A recipe for 4 people needs
1600 g of flour. How much
flour is needed for 6 people?

FLOUR

- Divide 1600g by 4, so 400g
  will be needed for 1 person.
- Multiply by 6, so 6 × 400g = 2400g will
  be needed for 6 people.

Example
A photocopier is set to reduce in the ratio of
3 : 5. What is the length of the reduced
diagram if the original is 12 cm?
- Divide 12 cm by 5. 12 ÷ 5 = 2.4 cm.
- Multiply this by 3 to get 3 × 2.4 = 7.2 cm.

 When answering problems that involve ratios, always work out what one share is worth. You should then be able to work out what any number of shares is worth.

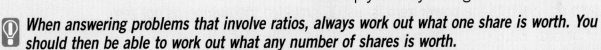

KEY TERMS

Make sure you
understand these
terms before moving on!
- enlarge
- ratio
- simplify

QUICK TEST

1. Write each of these ratios in its simplest form:
   a 12 : 15   b 6 : 12   c 25 : 10

2. Ahmed and Fiona share £500 between them in
   the ratio 2 : 3. How much does each receive?

3. A recipe for 12 people uses 500 g of plain
   flour. How much flour is needed for 18 people?

4. If 15 oranges cost £1.80, how much will 23
   identical oranges cost? (c)

5. The same brand of tuna fish is sold in two
   different-sized tins.
   Which tin represents
   the better value
   for money? (c)

48p

76p

TUNA

TUNA

198 g

240 g

Indices

An *index* is sometimes known as a *power*.

Powers

Examples

6^4 is read as '6 to the power of 4'. It means $6 \times 6 \times 6 \times 6$.

2^7 is read as '2 to the power 7'. It means $2 \times 2 \times 2 \times 2 \times 2 \times 2 \times 2$.

the *base* ⟶ a^b ⟵ the *index* or **power**

The **base** has to be the **same** when rules of indices are to be applied.

 Indices are a common topic on the non-calculator paper.

Rules of indices (Level 8)

You need to learn these rules:
- When **multiplying, add** the **indices**.
$$4^7 \times 4^3 = 4^{7+3} = 4^{10}$$
- When **dividing, subtract** the indices.
$$6^9 \div 6^4 = 6^{9-4} = 6^5$$
- When **raising one power to another, multiply** the indices.
$$(7^2)^4 = 7^{2 \times 4} = 7^8$$
- Anything raised to the **power zero** is just **1**, provided the number is not zero.
$$5^0 = 1 \qquad 6^0 = 1$$
$$2.7189^0 = 1 \qquad 0^0 \text{ is undefined (has no meaning).}$$
- Anything to the **power 1** is just **itself**.
$$15^1 = 15 \qquad 1923^1 = 1923$$
The above rules also apply when the indices are negative.

Examples

$6^{-2} \times 6^{12} = 6^{-2+12} = 6^{10}$ $\qquad$ $8^{-4} \times 8^{-3} = 8^{-4+-3} = 8^{-7}$

$(6^4)^{-2} = 6^{4 \times -2} = 6^{-8}$ $\qquad$ $5^0 = 1$

$5^7 \times 5^4 = 5^{7+4} = 5^{11}$ $\qquad$ $7^{-6} \div 7^{-2} = 7^{-6-(-2)} = 7^{-4}$

$9^4 \div 9 = 9^{4-1} = 9^3$ $\qquad$ $(12^3)^{-4} = 12^{3 \times -4} = 12^{-12}$

Indices and algebra (Level 8)

The rules that apply with numbers also apply with letters.

Laws of indices

$$a^n \times a^m = a^{n+m}$$

$$a^n \div a^m = a^{n-m}$$

$$(a^n)^m = a^{n \times m} = a^{nm}$$

$$a^0 = 1$$

$$a^1 = a$$

$$a^{-1} = \frac{1}{a}$$

💡 *Indices are becoming a very common topic on the non-calculator paper – learn the rules and you should be fine!*

Examples

Note that the numbers are multiplied...   ...but the powers of the same letter are added.

a $\quad 4x^2 \times 3x^5 = 12x^7$

b $\quad 12x^4 \div 3x^7 = 4x^{-3}$

c $\quad (7x^2)^2 = 49x^4$

d $\quad x^0 = 1$

e $\quad (2x^4)^3 = 8x^{12}$

Simplify $\quad \dfrac{3x^7 \times 4x^9}{6x^4} = \dfrac{12x^{16}}{6x^4} = 2x^{12}$

Work this out in 2 stages.

Simplify $\quad x^6 \times 4x^3 = 4x^9$

Simplify $\quad \dfrac{12a^2b^3}{6a^3b^2} = \dfrac{2b}{a} = 2a^{-1}b$

Simplify $\quad \dfrac{4a^4b^3}{2ab} = 2a^3b^2$

Simplify $\quad 12x^4y^2 \div 6x^5y^3 = 2x^{-1}y^{-1}$ or $\dfrac{2}{xy}$

Simplify $\quad \dfrac{3x^4 \times 5x^{-2}y^3}{15x^3y^2} = \dfrac{15x^2y^3}{15x^3y^2} = \dfrac{y}{x}$

KEY TERMS

Make sure you understand these terms before moving on!

- base
- index
- indices
- power

QUICK TEST

Level 8

1. Simplify the following.

   a $12^4 \times 12^8$ b $9^{-2} \times 9^{-4}$ c 4^0

   d $18^6 \div 18^{-2}$ e $(4^2)^5$ f 1^{20}

2. Simplify the following.

   a $x^4 \times x^9$ b $2x^6 \times 3x^7$ c $12x^4 \div 3x^2$

   d $25x^9 \div 5x^{-2}$ e $\dfrac{5x^6 \times 4x^9}{10x^3}$

Standard index form

Standard index form (Level 8) is used to write very large numbers or very small numbers in a simple way. When written in *standard form* the number will be written as:

$$a \times 10^n$$

a must be at least 1 but less than 10, $1 \leqslant a < 10$

The value of *n* is the *power* of 10 by which a must be multiplied to restore the number to its original value. You can think of it as the number of places the decimal point must 'move' to give the original number.

Learn these three rules

1 The number must always be at least 1 but less than 10

2 The power of 10, *n*, tells you how far the decimal point 'moves'

3 If the number is big *n* is positive. If the number is small *n* is negative.

Big numbers

Examples

a Write 6 230 000 in standard form.
Place the decimal point between the 6 and 2 to give 6.230000
$(1 \leqslant 6.23 < 10)$. Count how many places the decimal point needs to be 'moved' to restore the number.

6 2 3 0 0 0 0   (6 places)

In standard form:
$6 230 000 = 6.23 \times 10^6$

b $4371 = 4.371 \times 10^3$ in standard form.

Small numbers

Examples

a Write 0.003 71 in standard form.
Place the decimal point between the 3 and 7 to give 3.71 $(1 \leqslant 3.71 < 10)$. Count how many places the decimal point has been 'moved'.

0.0 0 3 7 1 (3 places)
In standard form:
$0.003 71 = 3.71 \times 10^{-3}$

This means that the decimal point is 'moved' 3 places to the left.

b $0.000 047 9 = 4.79 \times 10^{-5}$ in standard form.

Watch out!

Some common mistakes when answering standard form questions

■ Reading a calculator display such as $\boxed{2.4 \ ^{07}}$ incorrectly and writing down 2.47 instead of 2.4×10^7.

■ Forgetting to write the answer in standard form, particularly on the non-calculator paper, e.g. $(2 \times 10^6) \times (6 \times 10^3) = (2 \times 6) \times (10^6 \times 10^3)$

$$= 12 \times 10^9 \ ✗$$
$$= 1.2 \times 10^{10} \ ✓$$

Standard form and the calculator

To key a number in standard form into the calculator, use the $\boxed{\text{EXP}}$ key.
(Some calculators use $\boxed{\text{EE}}$. Check your calculator, as they vary greatly.)

Examples 6.23×10^6 can be keyed in as: $\boxed{6}\ \boxed{.}\ \boxed{2}\ \boxed{3}\ \boxed{\text{EXP}}\ \boxed{6}$

4.93×10^{-5} can be keyed in as: $\boxed{4}\ \boxed{.}\ \boxed{9}\ \boxed{3}\ \boxed{\text{EXP}}\ \boxed{5}\ \boxed{+/-}$

Most calculators do not show standard form correctly on the display.

$\boxed{\text{7.632 }^{09}}$ means 7.632×10^9. $\boxed{\text{4.62}^{-07}}$ means 4.62×10^{-7}.

Remember to put in the '$\times 10$' part if it has been left out.

Calculations with standard form

Use the calculator to do complex calculations in standard form.

💡 *It is important that you can do calculations with standard index form with and without a calculator as they could appear on both papers.*

Examples

$(2.6 \times 10^3) \times (8.9 \times 10^{12}) = 2.314 \times 10^{16}$ This would be keyed in as:

$\boxed{2}\ \boxed{.}\ \boxed{6}\ \boxed{\text{EXP}}\ \boxed{3}\ \boxed{\times}\ \boxed{8}\ \boxed{.}\ \boxed{9}\ \boxed{\text{EXP}}\ \boxed{1}\ \boxed{2}\ \boxed{=}$

Check that for $(1.8 \times 10^6) \div (2.7 \times 10^{-3})$ Just key in as normal:

the answer is 6.7×10^8 $\boxed{2}\ \boxed{.}\ \boxed{7}\ \boxed{\text{EXP}}\ \boxed{3}\ \boxed{+/-}$

If a calculation with standard form is on the non-calculator paper, you can use the laws of indices when multiplying and dividing numbers written in standard form.

Examples   **a** $(2.4 \times 10^{-4}) \times (3 \times 10^7)$

$= (2.4 \times 3) \times (10^{-4} \times 10^7)$

$= 7.2 \times (10^{-4+7})$

$= 7.2 \times 10^3$

b $(12.4 \times 10^{-4}) \div (4 \times 10^7)$

$= (12.4 \div 4) \times (10^{-4} \div 10^7)$

$= 3.1 \times (10^{-4-7})$

$= 3.1 \times 10^{-11}$

KEY TERMS

Make sure you understand these terms before moving on!

- index
- power
- standard form
- standard index form

QUICK TEST

1 Write the following numbers in standard form. (Level 8)
   a 630 000   b 2730   c 0.000 042 9   d 0.000 000 63

2 Without a calculator, work out the following, leaving your answers in standard form.
   a $(2 \times 10^5) \times (3 \times 10^7)$ b $(6.1 \times 10^{12}) \times (2 \times 10^{-4})$
   c $(8 \times 10^9) \div (2 \times 10^6)$ d $(6 \times 10^8) \div (2 \times 10^{-10})$

3 Work these out on a calculator. Give your answers to 3 significant figures. 🅒
   a $\dfrac{1.279 \times 10^9}{2.94 \times 10^{-2}}$ b $(1.693 \times 10^4) \times (2.71 \times 10^{12})$

4 Calculate, giving your answers in standard form correct to 3 significant figures. 🅒 $\dfrac{(3.72 \times 10^8) - (1.6 \times 10^4)}{3.81 \times 10^{-3}}$

Practice questions

Use the questions to test your progress.
Check your answers on page 95.

1. The temperature inside the house is 25°C higher than it is outside.
   If the temperature outside is –5°C, what is the temperature inside?

   30° × = 20 %

2. 1   2   3   4   5   6   7   8   9   10   11   12

   From the above numbers write down all the:

   a multiples of 4   *4, 8, 12* ✓   **b** prime numbers   *7* ✗

   c factors of 12   *3, 4, 1, 12* ✗ ✗

3. Write 24 as a product of prime factors.   *✗*

4. Work these out without using a calculator.   **a** $\sqrt{100}$ **b** 6^2 **c** $\sqrt{36}$ **d** 2^3

   10 ✓   *36* ✓   *6* ✓   *8* ✓

5. Matthew's calculator display shows 7.2^{-05} . Write down what the calculator display means.

   0.000072   0.000072 × 7.2 × 10⁻⁵

6. Work out the missing values.

   a $\frac{7}{12} = \frac{14}{x}$ **b** $\frac{125}{500} = \frac{y}{100}$ **c** $\frac{19}{38} = \frac{76}{z}$

   24 ✓   *25* ✓   *? × 152*

7. On a flag 27% is coloured red, 62% is blue and the rest is yellow. What percentage is yellow?

   62 + 27 = 89.   100 – 89 = 11 % ✗ *12 %*

8. If an apple costs 18p, work out the cost of 78 similar apples.

9. Jessica buys some tins of cat food at a total cost of £8.46. If each tin costs 47p, how many tins does Jessica buy?

10. Work out the numbers represented by the letters.

    a $11 + A = 6$ **b** $-8 + 7 = B$ **c** $-9 - C = 3$ **d** $10 - D = 3$

    11 – 6 = 5   –1   –12   7

11. A jumper costs £45. In a sale its price is reduced by 15%. What is its sale price?

    10 % = £4.50   5 % = £2.25   +   £6.75   £38.25

12. In an orchard there are 1600 apple and plum trees, divided in the ratio 3 : 5. How many apple trees are there in the orchard?

13. A house was bought for £75 000. Two years later it was sold for £93 000. Work out the percentage profit. **C**

14. A map is being enlarged in the ratio 12 : 7. If a road length was 21 cm on the original map, what is the length of the road on the enlarged map?

.... 36 cm ....

15. Work out the following. **a** $\frac{2}{5} + \frac{3}{10}$ **b** $\frac{2}{3} - 1\frac{3}{2}$ **c** $\frac{3}{10} \times \frac{5}{8}$ **d** $\frac{8}{9} \div 1\frac{1}{2}$ $\frac{2}{3}$

$\frac{7}{10}$ $\frac{1}{6}$ $\frac{15}{80}$ or $\frac{3}{16}$ $\frac{16}{27}$

16. Round the following to two decimal places.

   a 12.693   **b** 28.756   **c** 2.935   12.69   28.76   2.94

17. Round the following to three significant figures.

   a 273406   **b** 0.0007862   **c** 27050   273   0.000786   271

18. Complete the table.

Fraction	Decimal	Percentage
	0.25	25%
$\frac{5}{8}$		
	$0.\dot{6}$	66%

19. A car was bought for £8995. If the value of the car depreciates by 15% each year, how much will the car be worth after two years? **C**

....

20. Place these values in order, putting the smallest first. 61% 94% 0.93 $\frac{9}{10}$ $\frac{4}{7}$ 0.274

....

21. Without using a calculator, work out.

   a 6 × 0.001   **b** 400 × 0.01   **c** 50 ÷ 0.001

....

22. Work these out on your calculator: **C**

   a $\frac{57.5 \times 8.2}{10.3 + 11.5}$ **b** $\frac{(17.7)^3}{4.8 \times 3.3}$

....

23. Estimate the answer to $\frac{(16.57)^3 + 89}{7.7 \times 6.8}$.

....

24. (Level 8) The price of a CD player has been reduced in a sale by 15%. It now costs £320. What was the original price? **C**

....

25. (Level 8) Write these numbers in standard form:

   a 2670000   **b** 4270   **c** 0.03296   **c** 0.027

....

26. (Level 8) Work out the answers to these questions, giving your answers in standard form.

   a $(2 \times 10^9) \times (6 \times 10^{12})$ **b** $(8 \times 10^9) \div (4 \times 10^{-2})$

....

   A calculator may be used. (Level 8) This question is for level 8 students only. **C**

How well did you do? ✗ 1–6 Try again 7–13 Getting there 14–20 Good work 21–26 Excellent!

Algebra 1

Algebraic conventions

- In **algebra** letters represent numbers.
- A **term** is made up of numbers and letters multiplied together.
- An **expression** is made up of terms that are connected by +, – and may include brackets.

$$3xy - 5r + 2x^2 - 4$$

invisible + sign xy-term r-term x^2-term   number-term

There are several rules to follow when writing algebra.

$a + a + a + a = 4a$

$b \times b = b^2$ **not** $2b$

$b \times b \times b = b^3$ **not** $3b$

$n \times n \times 3 = 3n^2$ **not** $(3n)^{2s}$

$a \times 3 \times c = 3ac$

Put the number first and then the letters in alphabetical order; leave out the multiplication sign.

- When dividing, for example, $a \div 3$, write it as a fraction, $\dfrac{a}{3}$

Writing simple formulae

$n + 4$ is an expression. $y = n + 4$ is a **formula**, since it has an (=) sign in it.

Example

a How many blue tiles will there be in pattern number 4?

b Write down the formula for finding the number of tiles in pattern number n.

c How many tiles will be used in pattern number 12?

pattern number 1

pattern number 2

pattern number 3

pattern number 4

a Drawing the diagram. There are 16 blue tiles.

b Number of tiles $= 4 \times n + 1$

$= 4n + 1$

The $4n$ is the 4 lots of blue tiles.

The +1 is the yellow tile in the middle.

Remember to put an equals sign in your formula.

c If $n = 12$, i.e. number of tiles $= 4 \times 12 + 1 = 48 + 1 = 49$

Just substitute the value of n into the formula.

Using letters

Example

Emily plants potatoes, carrots and onions. m stands for the number of carrot seeds she plants. If she plants five more onion seeds than carrot seeds, how many onion seeds does she plant?

$m + 5$ This is an **expression**.

If she plants half as many onion seeds as carrot seeds, this is written as $m \div 2$, written as $\frac{m}{2}$.

> Algebra forms a large part of the SATS exam. Writing simple formulae as in the examples in this chapter is a very common topic – practise this type of question.

Example

Richard has p counters. David has three times as many counters. Write this as an expression.

- David has $3 \times p$ counters.
- $3 \times p$ is written as $3p$ in algebra; the multiplication sign is missed out.

> Remember that in algebra a division is usually written as a fraction, e.g. $x \div a = \frac{x}{a}$

Collecting like terms

- Expressions can be simplified by **collecting like terms**.
- In **like terms** the letters and powers are identical.

Examples

$3p + 2p = 5p$

$6a + 2c$ cannot be simplified

$5n + 2n - 6n = n$

$2a + 4b + 3a - 2b = 5a + 2b$

   Remember to include the sign. 5a + 2b, **not** 5a 2b.

$5xy + 2yx = 7xy$

Multiplying letters and numbers

- Algebraic expressions are often simplified by multiplying them together, e.g. $5a \times 2b = 10ab$.
- When multiplying expressions, multiply the numbers together, then the letters together.

Examples Simplify these expressions:

Multiply the numbers

Multiply the letters

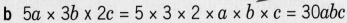

a $3a \times 4b = 3 \times 4 \times a \times b = 12ab$

b $5a \times 3b \times 2c = 5 \times 3 \times 2 \times a \times b \times c = 30abc$

c $2a \times 3a = 2 \times 3 \times a \times a = 6a^2$

> There are a lot of rules and techniques to learn. When substituting values into formulae, be sure to do it carefully and show full working.

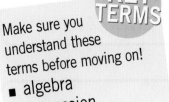

KEY TERMS

Make sure you understand these terms before moving on!

- algebra
- expression
- formula
- like term
- term

QUICK TEST

❶ The diagram shows some patterns made from sticks. If P represents the pattern number and S represents the number of sticks, write down a formula connecting S and P.

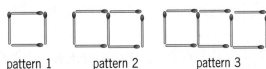

pattern 1   pattern 2   pattern 3

❷ Write these expressions as simply as possible.

a 6 more than n b 4 less than p
c 6 more than 3 lots of y
d h divided by 7   e 5 less than n divided by p

Algebra 2

Substituting values into expressions and formulae

Replacing a letter with a number is called **substitution**. When substituting:

- Write out the expression first, then replace the letters with the values given
- Work out the value on your calculator. Use brackets keys where possible and **pay attention to order of operations**.

Examples

If $a = 2$, $b = 4.1$, $c = -3$, $d = 5$, find the value of these expressions, giving your answer to 1 decimal place.

a $\dfrac{a + b}{2}$ **b** $\dfrac{a^2 + c^2}{d}$

c ab **d** $3d - ab$

Remember to show the substitution.

a $\dfrac{a + b}{2} = \dfrac{2 + 4.1}{2} = 3.05 = 3.1$ (1 d.p.)

b $\dfrac{a^2 + c^2}{d} = \dfrac{2^2 + (-3)^2}{5} = 2.6$ You may need to treat c^2 as $(-3)^2$

c $ab = 2 \times 4.1 = 8.2$

   ab means $a \times b$.

d $3d - ab = (3 \times 5) - (2 \times 4.1) = 6.8$

Multiplying out single brackets

- Multiply everything inside the brackets by everything outside the brackets.

Examples $2(a + b) = 2a + 2b$ $3(x - 2) = 3x - 6$ The multiplication sign is not shown.

$a(b + d) = ab + ad$ $r(3r - 2s) = 3r^2 - 2rs$ Remember $r \times r = r^2$

This is known as expanding brackets. If the term outside the brackets is **negative**, all of the signs of the terms inside the brackets are changed when multiplying out.

Examples $-2(a + b) = -2a - 2b$ $-a(a - b) = -a^2 + ab$ Remember that $-(a + b)$ means $-1 \times (a + b)$.

To simplify expressions, expand the brackets first, then **collect like terms**.

Example $3(a + 1) + 2(a + b) = 3a + 3 + 2a + 2b$ Multiply out brackets.

     $= 5a + 2b + 3$ Collect like terms.

Multiplying out two brackets

Each term in the first brackets is multiplied with each term in the second brackets.

Examples   **a** $(x + 2)(x + 3) = x(x + 3) + 2(x + 3)$ **b** $(x + 4)^2 = (x + 4)(x + 4)$

     $= x^2 + 3x + 2x + 6$ $= x(x + 4) + 4(x + 4)$

     $= x^2 + 5x + 6$ $= x^2 + 4x + 4x + 16$

     $= x^2 + 8x + 16$

A common error is to think that $(x + 4)^2$ means $x^2 + 4^2$ i.e. $x^2 + 16$

Factorising (putting brackets in)

This is the reverse of expanding brackets. An **expression** is put into brackets by taking out common factors.

expanding

$2(x + 4)$ → $2x + 8$

factorising

Examples

a $5x + 10 = 5(x + 2)$

b $8x - 16 = 8(x - 2)$

c $3x + 9 = 3(x + 3)$

💡 *Remember to take out the highest factor.*

Factorising a Quadratic expression (level 8)

A **quadratic** expression of the type $x^2 + bx + c$ may be factorised.

expanding

$(x + 2)(x + 1)$ → $x^2 + 3x + 2$

factorising

The 2 and the 1 multiply to give 2, and add to give 3 in $3x$.

Examples

a $x^2 + 5x - 6 = (x - 1)(x + 6)$

b $x^2 - 6x + 8 = (x - 2)(x - 4)$

c $x^2 - 16 = (x - 4)(x + 4)$ ← This is the difference of two squares.

Rearranging a formula

The **subject** of a formula is the letter that appears on its own on one side of the formula. The **balancing method** can be used to rearrange the formula.

Example Make x the subject of each formula.

a $y = \dfrac{x}{4} + 6$

$y - 6 = \dfrac{x}{4}$ Subtract 6 from both sides

$4(y - 6) = x$ Multiply both sides by 4

b $y = 5(x - 2)$

$\dfrac{y}{5} = (x - 2)$ Divide both sides by 5.

$\dfrac{y}{5} + 2 = x$ Add 2 to both sides.

QUICK TEST

1 Some cards have the following expressions written on them. Which card is the same as $4(a + 2)$?
A $2a + 8$ **B** $2a + 4$ **C** $4a + 8$ **D** $4a + 2$

2 If $a = 3$, $b = 2.1$, $c = -4$, work out the answer to these expressions, giving your answer to 1 dp. ©
a $3a + 2b$ **b** $5c - 2a$ **c** abc

3 Expand these brackets and simplify.
a $2(x - 3)$ **b** $(x - 2)(x + 1)$ **c** $(x - 1)(x - 4)$

4 Factorise each expression.
a $5x - 25$ **b** $12x - 20$ **c** $4y + 16$

5 Rearrange to make x the subject.
a $y = 5x - 2$ **b** $y = \dfrac{3x + 4}{7}$ **c** $y = \dfrac{x}{3} + 2$

6 Factorise the following expressions.
a $n^2 + 2n + 1$ **a** $n^2 - 5n + 6$ **a** $n^2 - 25$

Equations 1

Solving simple linear equations

- An **equation** involves an **unknown value** that has to be worked out.
- The **balance method** is usually used; whatever is done to one side of an equation must be done to the other.

Examples

Solve the following. **a** $n - 4 = 6$ **b** $n + 2 = 8$ **c** $5n = 20$ **d** $\frac{n}{3} = 2$

a $n - 4 = 6$

$\quad\quad n = 6 + 4$ Add 4 to both sides.

$\quad\quad n = 10$

b $n + 2 = 8$

$\quad\quad n = 8 - 2$ Subtract 2 from both sides.

$\quad\quad n = 6$

c $5n = 20$

$\quad\quad n = \frac{20}{5}$ Divide both sides by 5.

$\quad\quad n = 4$

d $\frac{n}{3} = 2$

$\quad\quad n = 2 \times 3$ Multiply both sides by 3.

$\quad\quad n = 6$

💡 **Show all working and do the calculation step by step.**

Solving equations of the form $ax + b = c$

Examples Solve these equations. **a** $5n + 1 = 11$ **b** $\frac{n}{3} + 1 = 4$

a $5n + 1 = 11$ Subtract 1 from both sides.

$\quad\quad 5n = 11 - 1$

$\quad\quad 5n = 10$

$\quad\quad n = \frac{10}{5} = 2$ Divide both sides by 5.

b $\frac{n}{3} + 1 = 4$

$\quad\quad \frac{n}{3} = 4 - 1$

$\quad\quad \frac{n}{3} = 3$

$\quad\quad n = 3 \times 3$ Multiply both sides by 3.

$\quad\quad n = 9$

💡 *Equations are very popular on the SATS paper – try to work through them in a logical way, showing full working. If you have time, check your answer by substituting it back into the original equation.*

Solving linear equations of the form $ax + b = cx + d$

For **linear** equations you need to get the xs together on one side of the equals sign and the numbers on the other side.

Example

Solve the equation $7x - 2 = 2x + 13$

$$7x - 2 = 2x + 13$$
$$7x - 2 - 2x = 13 \qquad \text{Subtract } 2x \text{ from both sides.}$$
$$5x = 13 + 2 \qquad \text{Add 2 to both sides.}$$
$$5x = 15$$
$$x = \frac{15}{5} = 3$$

Solving linear equations with brackets

Just because an equation has **brackets** don't be put off – the method is just the same as for the other equations once the brackets have been multiplied out.

Examples Solve these equations:

$$5(2x - 1) = 10$$
$$10x - 5 = 10 \qquad \text{Multiply brackets out first.}$$
$$10x = 10 + 5$$
$$10x = 15$$
$$x = \frac{15}{10} = 1.5$$

$$4(2n + 5) = 3(n + 10)$$
$$8n + 20 = 3n + 30 \qquad \text{Multiply brackets out first.}$$
$$8n + 20 - 3n = 30$$
$$5n = 30 - 20$$
$$5n = 10 \qquad \text{Solve as before.}$$
$$n = \frac{10}{5} = 2$$

KEY TERMS

Make sure you understand these terms before moving on!
- balance method
- brackets
- equation
- linear
- unknown value

QUICK TEST

Solve the following equations.

1. $2x = 10$
2. $2x - 3 = 9$
3. $4x + 1 = 8$
4. $5x + 3 = 2x + 9$
5. $6x - 1 = 2x + 15$
6. $3(x + 2) = x + 4$
7. $2(x - 1) = 12(x + 1)$

Equations 2

Simultaneous equations

Two equations with two unknowns are called **simultaneous equations**.
They can be solved in several ways. Solving equations simultaneously involves finding values for the letters that will make both equations work.

Graphical method

The point at which any two lines **intersect** represent the simultaneous solutions of these equations.

Example Solve the simultaneous equations: $y = 2x - 3$, $y - x = 1$ by a **graphical method**.

- Draw the two graphs

$y = 2x - 3$ If $x = 0$, $y = -3$
          If $y = 0$, $x = \frac{3}{2}$

$y - x = 1$ If $x = 0$, $y = 1$
          If $y = 0$, $x = -1$

Work out the **coordinates** when $x = 0$ and when $y = 0$ to draw a quick graph.

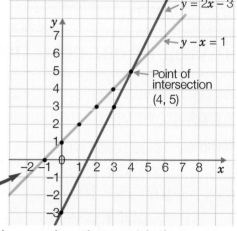

- At the **point of intersection** $x = 4$ and $y = 5$.

Elimination method

The **coefficient** is the number that multiplies a letter, e.g. the coefficient of $-3x$ is -3.

- If the **coefficient** of one of the letters is the same in both equations, then that letter may be **eliminated** by subtracting the equations. Otherwise you may need to multiply one or both equations so that the coefficients of one of the unknowns are the same.

Example Solve simultaneously $n + 3p = 25$, $2n + p = 15$.

$n + 3p = 25$ **1**   Label the equations **1** and **2**.
$2n + p = 15$ **2**   As no coefficients match, multiply equation **2** by 3.
$6n + 3p = 45$ **3**   The coefficients of p are now the same in equations **1** and **3**.
$5n + 0p = 20$ Subtract equation **1** from equation **3**.
  So $5n = 20$
    $n = 4$

$2n + p = 15$ **Substitute** the value of $n = 4$ into equation **1** or **2**.
so $8 + p = 15$
    $p = 7$ Always check that the values work.

Check in equation **1** $4 + 3 \times 7 = 25$ ✔
(Substitute $n = 4$ and $p = 7$ into the other equation.)
The solution is $n = 4$ and $p = 7$.

To eliminate terms with opposite signs add.
To eliminate terms with the same signs subtract.

💡 *Simultaneous equations are usually a difficult topic to master. Try to learn the steps outlined above and practise with lots of examples. Use the check at the end to make sure you have got the answer right.*

Using equations to solve problems

Example

Class 9A were playing a number game. Saima said, 'Multiplying my number by 5 and adding 8 gives the same answer as subtracting my number from 20.'

a Call Saima's number y and form an equation.

b Solve the equation to work out Saima's number.

a $\quad 5y + 8 = 20 - y$

b $\quad 5y + 8 = 20 - y$

$5y + 8 + y = 20$

$6y = 20 - 8$

$6y = 12$

$y = \dfrac{12}{6} = 2$

Saima's number is 2.

 Check at the end that $y = 2$ works in the equation.

Example

The lengths of the sides of the triangle are given in the diagram.

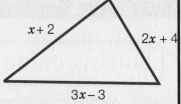

a Write down an expression for the perimeter of the triangle.

b If the perimeter of the triangle is 39 cm, form an equation and solve it to find the length of each side.

a Perimeter $= (x + 2) + (3x - 3) + (2x + 4)$

$\qquad\qquad = 6x + 3$ The perimeter is found by adding the three lengths.

b $6x + 3 = 39$

$6x = 39 - 3$

$6x = 36$

$x = \dfrac{36}{6}$ $\quad \therefore x = 6$

The sides are $\quad x + 2 = 8$ cm

$2x + 4 = 16$ cm

$3x - 3 = 15$ cm

KEY TERMS

Make sure you understand these terms before moving on!

- coefficient
- coordinates
- elimination method
- graphical method
- intersect
- point of intersection
- simultaneous equations
- substitute

QUICK TEST

❶ Solve the following pairs of simultaneous equations:

a $\quad 4x + 7y = 10$
$\quad 2x + 3y = 3$

b $\quad 3a - 5b = 1$
$\quad 2a + 3b = 7$

❷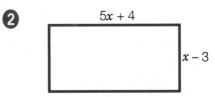

a Write down an equation for the perimeter of the rectangle above, if the perimeter is 74 cm.

b Solve the equation to find the length and width of the rectangle.

EQUATIONS 2 Algebra

Inequalities

Solving cubic equations by trial and improvement

In the method of **trial and improvement**, successive approximations are made in order to get closer to the correct value.

Example

The equation $x^3 - 5x = 10$ has a **solution** between 2 and 3.
Find this solution to two decimal places.
Draw a table to help.
Substitute different values of x into $x^3 - 5x$.

x	$x^3 - 5x$	Comment
2.5	3.125	too small
2.8	7.952	too small
2.9	9.889	too small
2.95	10.922375	too big
2.94	10.712184	too big
2.91	10.092171	too big

At this stage the solution is trapped between 2.90 and 2.91.
Checking the middle value $x = 2.905$ gives $x^3 - 5x = 9.99036...$ which is too small.

2.90	2.905	2.91
(too small)	(too small)	(too big)

The diagram makes it clear that the solution is 2.91 correct to two decimal places.

💡 *When solving equations by trial and improvement it is the value of x you must give as the solution.*

The four inequality symbols

> means 'greater than'   ≥ means 'greater than or equal to'
< means 'less than'   ≤ means 'less than or equal to'
So $x > 3$ and $3 < x$ both say 'x is greater than 3'.

Solving inequalities

Inequalities are solved in a similar way to equations.

Multiplying and dividing by **negative numbers** changes the **direction** of the sign. For example if $-x \geqslant 5$ then $x \leqslant -5$.

Examples

Solve the following inequalities.

a $4x - 2 < 2x + 6$

b $-5 < 3x + 1 \leqslant 13$

a $4x - 2 < 2x + 6$ Subtract $2x$ from both sides.

   $2x - 2 < 6$ Add 2 to both sides.

     $2x < 8$ Divide both sides by 2.

       $x < 4$

The solution of the inequality may be represented on a number line.

> Use ● when the end point is included and ○ when the end point is not included.

b $-5 < 3x + 1 \leqslant 13$ Subtract 1 from each part.

   $-6 < 3x \leqslant 12$ Divide by 3.

   $-2 < x \leqslant 4$

The **integer values** which satisfy the above inequality are $-1, 0, 1, 2, 3, 4$.

 Inqualities are solved in a similar way to equations.

Graphs of inequalities (Level 8)

The graph of an equation such as $y = 3$ is a line, whereas the graph of the inequality $y < 3$ is a **region** with the line $y = 3$ as its **boundary**.

To show the region for given inequalities:

- Draw the boundary lines first.
- For **strict** inequalities > and <, the boundary line is not included and is shown as a dotted line.
- It is often easier with several inequalities to shade out the unwanted regions, so that the solution is shown **unshaded**.

Example The diagram shows unshaded the region $x > 1$, $x + y \leqslant 4$, $y \geqslant 0$.

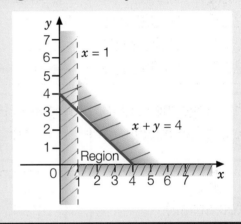

Make sure you understand these terms before moving on!

KEY TERMS

- <
- ≤
- boundary
- inequality
- integer value
- >
- ≥
- region
- solution
- substitute
- trial and improvement

❶ If $12x - x^2 = 34$ has a solution between 4 and 5, use trial and improvement to find the value of x to 1 decimal place. **c**

❷ Solve the following inequalities:

   a $2x - 3 < 9$ b $5x + 1 \geqslant 21$

   c $1 \leqslant 3x - 2 \leqslant 7$ d $1 \leqslant 5x + 2 < 12$

Patterns & sequences

Number patterns and sequences

- A **sequence** is a list of numbers. There is usually a relationship between the numbers. Each number in the list is called a **term**.
- There are lots of different **number patterns**. When finding a missing number in the number pattern it is sensible to see what is happening in the gap.

Examples

The odd numbers have a **common difference** of two.

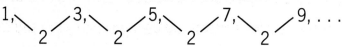

The rule is **add 2 each time**.

The next term in this sequence is found by multiplying the previous term by 3.

2, $\xrightarrow{\times 3}$ 6, $\xrightarrow{\times 3}$ 18, $\xrightarrow{\times 3}$ 54, . . .

The next term in this sequence is found by adding the two previous terms. It is known as the Fibonacci sequence.

1, 1, 2, 3, 5, 8, 13

$\underbrace{\quad}_{1+1}$ $\underbrace{\quad}_{2+3}$ $\underbrace{\quad}_{5+8}$

Dividing by 2, 5 and 10

One number is **divisible** by another if there is no remainder.

Example

4 is divisible by 2,
   $4 \div 2 = 2$
7 is not divisible by 2,
   $7 \div 2 = 3.5$

- A number is divisible by 2 if it is an even number.
- A number is divisible by 5 if it ends in 0 or 5.
- A number is divisible by 10 if it ends in 0.

Finding the nth term of a linear sequence

- The nth term is often shown as U_n, so the 12th term is U_{12}.
- For a **linear** sequence the nth term takes the form of $U_n = an + b$. The gap or difference gives the value of a.

Example

Find the nth term of this sequence. 4, 7, 10, 13, 16

- Look at the differences between the terms. If they are the same this gives the multiple or a.
- Adjust the rule by adding or taking away.

term	1	2	3	4	5	... n
sequence	4	7	10	13	16	

    3   3   3   3

The multiple is 3, giving $3n$.
The multiple is 3, so 3n will be in each term.
If n is 1, $3 \times 1 = 3$ but the first term is 4 so add 1.
nth term $U_n = 3n + 1$.

Check your rule with the second term to make sure it works.

Common number patterns

1, 4, 9, 16, 25, ...	**Square numbers**
1, 8, 27, 64, 125, ...	Cube numbers
1, 3, 6, 10, 15, ...	Triangular numbers
1, 1, 2, 3, 5, 8, 13, ...	Fibonacci sequence
2, 4, 8, 16, 32, 64, ...	Powers of 2
10, 100, 1000, 10000, 100000, ...	Powers of 10

💡 *These number patterns are common and you need to remember them.*

Finding the nth term of a quadratic sequence

In a **quadratic** sequence the first differences are **not** constant but the second differences are.

The nth term takes the form of $U_n = an^2 + bn + c$, where b and c may be zero.

Example For the sequence of square numbers find an expression for the nth term.

$$1 \quad 4 \quad 9 \quad 16 \quad 25$$

First differences → $3 \quad 5 \quad 7 \quad 9$

Second differences → $2 \quad 2 \quad 2$

- Since the second differences are the same, the rule for the nth term is quadratic.
- The nth term is n^2.

Example Find the nth term of this sequence.

$$3 \quad 9 \quad 19 \quad 33 \quad 51$$

First differences → $6 \quad 10 \quad 14 \quad 18$

Second differences → $4 \quad 4 \quad 4$

- Since the second differences are the same then the rule for the nth term is quadratic.
- The **coefficient** of n^2 is $\dfrac{\text{(second difference)}}{2} = 4 \div 2 = 2$
- Adjusting as before gives $2n^2 + 1$.

💡 *Finding the nth term is a very useful method since it helps you to find a formula when given a sequence of values. You must take care though when finding the nth term of a quadratic sequence since they are more difficult.*

KEY TERMS

Make sure you understand these terms before moving on!

- coefficient
- common difference
- linear
- number pattern
- quadratic
- second difference
- sequence
- square numbers
- term

QUICK TEST

Find the nth term of each of these sequences.

1
a 3, 7, 11, 15, 19
b 8, 11, 14, 17, 20
c 2, 5, 10, 17, 26

2 Find the next two numbers in this sequence.
32, 16, 8, 4,___, ___,

Coordinates & graphs

Coordinates

- **Coordinates** are used to locate the position of a point on a **graph**.
- When reading coordinates, read across first, then up or down.
- Coordinates are always written inside brackets, with a comma in between, for example (2, 4).
- The horizontal axis is the x-axis. The vertical axis is the y-axis.

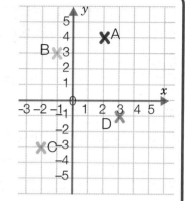

Examples

A has coordinates (2, 4)   B has coordinates (–1, 3)
C has coordinates (–2, –3)   D has coordinates (3, –1)

Make sure you write the brackets and comma.
Remember to read across first, then up or down.

Graphs of the form $y = a$, $x = b$

Example
Draw the line $y = 3$. Draw the line $x = 2$.

$y = a$ is a horizontal line with every y-coordinate equal to a.
$x = b$ is a vertical line with every x-coordinate equal to b.

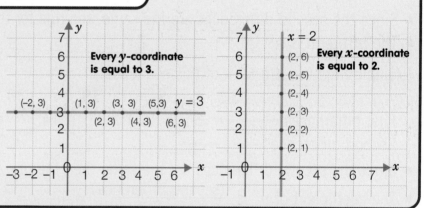

Finding the gradient of a straight line

- To find the **gradient**, choose two points.
- Draw a triangle as shown.
- Find the change in y (height) and the change in x (base).

- Gradient = $\dfrac{\text{change in } y}{\text{change in } x}$ or $\dfrac{\text{height}}{\text{base}} = \dfrac{4}{3} = 1\dfrac{1}{3}$

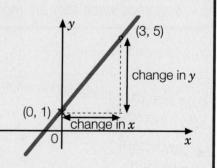

- Decide if the gradient is positive or negative.

💡 *Do not just count the squares as the scales may be different.*

Graphs of the form $y = mx + c$

These are straight-line (linear) graphs.
The general equation of a straight line
graph is $y = mx + c$.
m is the gradient (steepness) of the line.
c is the **intercept** on the y-axis, where the
graph cuts the y-axis.
Parallel lines have the **same** gradient.

> 🛈 **To work out the coordinates for the graph
> you can either draw up a table as shown in
> the examples, or use a function machine or
> mapping diagrams.**
>
> **Once you have plotted the coordinates,
> check they are on a straight line. If not, go
> back and check the coordinates have been
> worked out properly.**

Example

Draw the graphs of $y = 2x$, $y = -2x$, $y = 3x$
and $y = x - 2$ on the same axes.

- Work out coordinates for each graph.

$y = 2x$

x	-2	-1	0	1	2
y	-4	-2	0	2	4

$y = -2x$

x	-2	-1	0	1	2
y	4	2	0	-2	-4

$y = 3x$

x	-2	-1	0	1	2
y	-6	-3	0	3	6

$y = x - 2$

x	-2	-1	0	1	2
y	-4	-3	-2	-1	0

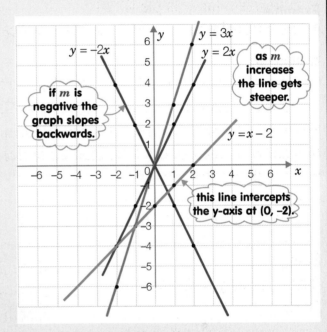

- Plot each set of coordinates and join up the points with a straight line.
- Label each of the graphs.

KEY TERMS

Make sure you understand these terms before moving on!

- coordinate
- gradient
- graph
- intercept
- $y = mx + c$

QUICK TEST

1. The graph of $y = x - 1$ is drawn on the graph opposite.

   a Draw the following graphs on the same axes.

   i $y = 2x$ **ii** $y = 4x$

   b What do you notice about the graphs of $y = 2x$ and $y = 4x$?

   c Without working out any coordinates draw the graph of $y = x - 2$.

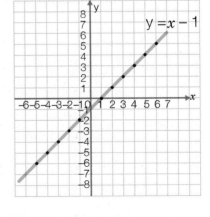

43

More graphs

Graphs of the form $y = ax^2 + bx + c$

They are often known as **parabolas**.

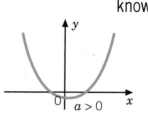
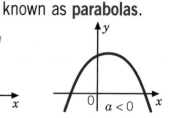

These are called **quadratic** graphs where $a \neq 0$.
These graphs are curved.
If $a > 0$ then the graph is U-shaped.
If $a < 0$ then the graph is an upside-down U.

Example

Draw the graph of $y = x^2 - x - 6$ using values of x from –2 to 3.
Use the graph to find the value of x when $y = -3$.

■ Make a table of values.

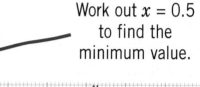
Work out $x = 0.5$ to find the minimum value.

x	–2	–1	0	1	2	3	0.5
y	0	–4	–6	–6	–4	0	–6.25

■ To work out the values of y, substitute the values
  of x into the equation:
  If $x = 1$ $\quad y = x^2 - x - 6$
  $\quad\quad\quad\quad = 1^2 - 1 - 6 = -6$

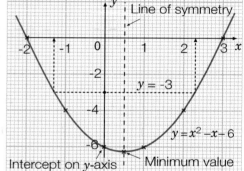

■ Don't try to key this all into your calculator at
  once. Do it step by step.
■ Plot the points and join them with a smooth curve.
■ The **minimum value** is when $x = 0.5$, $y = -6.25$.
■ The line of **symmetry** is at $x = 0.5$.
■ The curve cuts the y-axis at $(0, -6)$, or $(0, c)$.

Show clearly on your graph
how you take your readings.

■ When $y = -3$, read across from $y = -3$ to the graph then read up to the x-axis. $x = 2.3$
  and $x = -1.3$. These are the approximate solutions of the equation $x^2 - x - 6 = -3$.

The graph of $y = x^3$ (Level 8)

When asked to draw the graph of $y = x^3$, follow
the methods as shown before.
■ Work out the y-**coordinate** for each point.
■ Replace x in the equation with the coordinate.

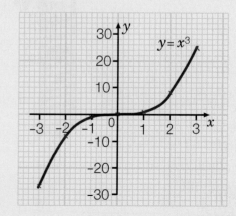

x	–3	–2	–1	0	1	2	3
y	–27	–8	–1	0	1	8	27

■ Plot the x- and y-coordinates from the
  table above.
■ Notice the shape of the graph of $y = x^3$.

Remember: $x^3 = x \times x \times x$.

Graphs involving $\frac{1}{x}$ (Level 8)

An equation of the form $y = \frac{a}{x}$ takes two basic forms, depending on the value of a.

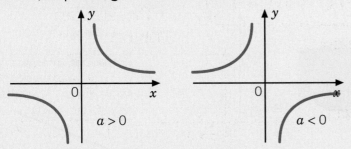

$a > 0$ $a < 0$

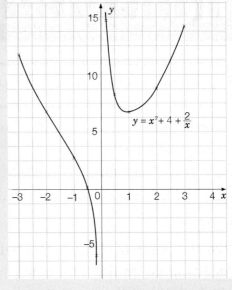

$y = x^2 + 4 + \frac{2}{x}$

Example

Draw the graph of $y = x^2 + 4 + \frac{2}{x}$ for $-3 \leqslant x \leqslant 3$.

■ Make a table of values:

There is no 0 column since you cannot calculate $\frac{2}{x}$ if $x = 0$.

x	-3	-2	-1	-0.5	-0.2	0.2	0.5	1	2	3
x^2	9	4	1	0.25	0.04	0.04	0.25	1	4	9
$+4$	4	4	4	4	4	4	4	4	4	4
$+\frac{2}{x}$	$-0.\dot{6}$	-1	-2	-4	-10	10	4	2	1	$0.\dot{6}$
y	$12.\dot{3}$	7	3	0.25	-5.96	14.04	8.25	7	9	$13.\dot{6}$

■ Plot the points and draw a smooth curve.
  There will be a break in the curve at $x = 0$.

QUICK TEST

❶ Draw the graph of $y = 2x^2 + 1$ for values of x from -3 to 3. Complete the table of values first.

x	-3	-2	-1	0	1	2	3
y	19						

❷ (Level 8) Match each of the four graphs below with one of the following equations.

a $y = 2x - 5$ b $y = x^2 + 3$ c $y = 3 - x^2$
d $y = 5 - x$ e $y = x^3$ f $y = \frac{2}{x}$

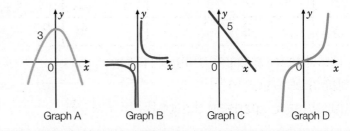

Graph A   Graph B   Graph C   Graph D

Interpreting graphs

Using Linear Graphs

- **Linear** graphs are often used to show **relationships**.

Examples The graph shows the charges made by a van hire firm.

- Point A shows the basic charge for hiring the van, which is £50.
- The **gradient** shows that £20 was then charged per day. Hence for 5 days' hire, the van cost £50 + £20 × 5 = £150.

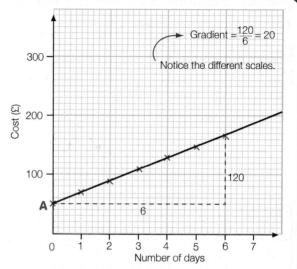

Gradient $= \frac{120}{6} = 20$

Notice the different scales.

Distance–time graphs

These are often known as **travel graphs**. The speed of an object can be found by finding the gradient of the line.

$$\text{speed} = \frac{\text{distance travelled}}{\text{time taken}}$$

Example The graph shows Mr Rogers' car journey. Work out the speed of each stage.

a The car is travelling at 30 mph for 1 hour (30 ÷ 1).

b The car is stationary for 30 minutes.

c The graph is steeper so the car is travelling faster, at a speed of 60 mph for 30 minutes (30 ÷ 0.5).

d The car is stationary for 1 hour.

e The return journey is at a speed of 40 mph (60 ÷ 1.5).

Notice the importance of using the gradient of a line. It is useful to note that on the distance–time graph example, the scales on both axes are different. You must take care when reading the scales: always make sure you understand the scales before you start.

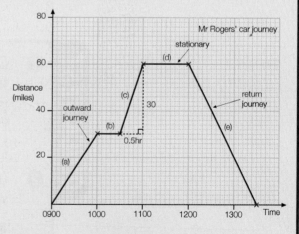

When answering questions involving distance–time graphs try to keep the following in mind.

The steeper the graph the greater the speed. Object A is travelling faster than object B which in turn is travelling faster than object C

The green line shows an incorrect journey home because you cannot go back in time

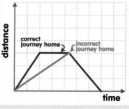

Conversion graphs

Conversion graphs are used to convert values of one quantity to another, e.g. litres to pints, kilometres to miles, pounds to dollars.

Example

Suppose £1 is worth \$1.50. Draw a conversion graph.

multiply by 1.5

£1   \$1.50

divide by 1.5

£	1	2	3	4	5
\$	1.5	3	4.5	6	7.5

× 1.5

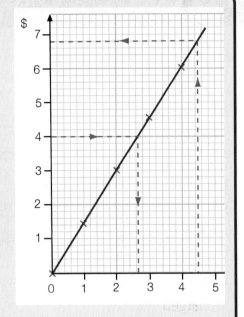

- Make a table of values.
- Plot each of these points on the graph paper.
- To change \$ to £, read across to the line then down, e.g. \$4 is £2.67 (approx.)
- To change £ to \$, read up to the line then read across, e.g. £4.50 is \$6.80 (approx.)

1 These containers are being filled with a liquid at a **rate** of 150 ml per second. The graphs show how the depth of the water changes with time. Match the containers with the graphs.

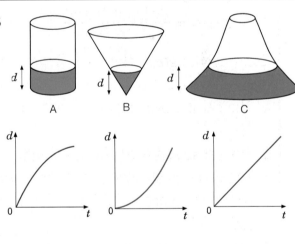

KEY TERMS

Make sure you understand these terms before moving on!
- conversion graph
- gradient
- linear
- rate
- relationship
- travel graph

2 The distance–time graph shows Mrs Roberts' car journey.

a At what speed did she travel for the first 2 hours?

b What is Mrs Roberts doing at A?

c At what speed is her return journey?

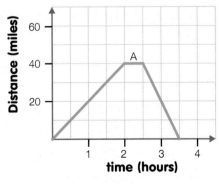

Practice questions

Use the questions to test your progress. Check your answers on page 95.

1. A shape has the lengths shown in the diagram. Write down an expression for the perimeter of the shape.

   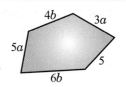

   5 + 8a + 10b

2. Here is a pattern made up of regular hexagons of side length 1 cm.

   a Complete this table showing the pattern number and perimeter of the shapes.

   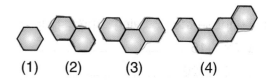

   (1)   (2)   (3)   (4)

Pattern number (n)	1	2	3	4	5	6
Perimeter of shape (p)	6	*10*	14	*18*	*22*	*26*

   b Write down a formula that connects the perimeter (p) and the pattern number (n).

3. If $a = 3$, $b = 2$ and $c = -1$, calculate the value of each of the following.

   a $a + b + c$ *3 + 2 + -1 = 4*

   b $2a - 3b$ *2 × 3 - 3 × 2   6 - 6 = 0*

   c $5a - 2c$ *5 × 3 - 2 × 2   15 - 4 = 11*

   d $a^2 + c^2 - 2b$ *3 × 3 + -1 × -1 - 2 × 2*

4. Using the formula $v = u + at$, calculate the value of:

   a v when $u = 200$, $a = 30$ $t = 4$ *v = 200 + 30 × 4   v = 200 + 120   v = 320*

   b v when $u = 500$, $a = 40$ $t = 10$ *v = 500 + 40 × 10   v = 500 + 400   v = 900*

5. Some cards have the following expressions on them.

   | $2n + 8$ | n^2 | $2n + 4$ | $2n$ | $5n$ | $4n + 8$ | $2n - 2$ | $2n - 1$ | $n + n$ | $4n + 2$ |

   Which cards are the same as:

   a $4(n + 2)$ ....

   b $n \times n$ ....

   c $2(n - 1)$ ....

   d $2n + 2n - 3 + 5$ ....

6. Solve the following equations.

   a $5a + 10 = 15$ ....

   b $\dfrac{n}{5} - 1 = 6$ ....

7. The graph of $y = x - 2$ is drawn on the graph opposite. Draw the following graphs on the same axes.

   a $y = 2x$ **b** $y = 3x$

   c What do you notice about the graphs of $y = 2x$ and $y = 3x$?

   ....

   d Without working out any coordinates, draw the graph of $y = 2x - 4$.

   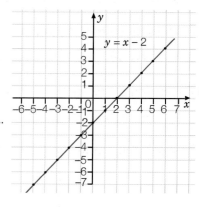

8. Solve the following equations.

   a $6n + 2 = 4n + 8$ ....

   b $6(n + 2) = 5n + 7$ ....

   c $2(n - 1) = 3(n + 4)$ ....

9. A rectangle has a length of $(2n + 1)$ cm and a width of 4 cm.

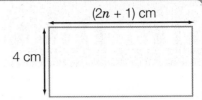

(2n + 1) cm

4 cm

 a Write an expression for the perimeter of the rectangle.
 Simplify as much as possible.

 ....

 b If the perimeter of the rectangle is 22 cm, write an equation involving n and solve it to find the value of n.

 ....

10. Write down the nth term of the following sequence.

 5, 7, 9, 11, 13, ...

11. Factorise the following expressions:

 a $5x + 15$ .... **b** $6x - 12$ ....

 c $12x + 20$ .... **d** $n^2 + 5n + 4$ .... (Level 8)

 e $n^2 - 8n + 12n$ .... (Level 8)

12. For each function write down the gradient and intercept of the graph:

 a $y = 4x + 10$ .... **b** $y = 6 - 2x$ ....

13. The travel graph shows the car journeys of two people. From the travel graph find:

 a the speed at which Miss Young is travelling

 b the length of time Mr Price has a break

 c the speed of Mr Price from London to Birmingham

 d the time at which Miss Young and Mr Price pass each other.

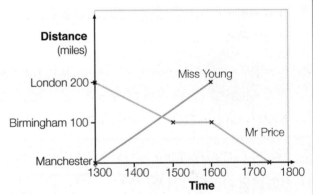

14. Solve these simultaneous equations. $2x + 3y = 6$ $x + y = 1$

 ....

15. Solve these inequalities and represent the solution on a number line:

 a $3n + 2 < 6$ ....

 b $5n - 1 \leq 2n + 5$ ....

16. Write down the nth term of this sequence:

 3, 6, 11, 18, ...

17. Rearrange the formula to make x the subject:

 $y = \dfrac{x}{3} - 6$ ....

18. Match the graphs with the equations. i) $y = x^2 - 4$ ii) $y = 2x + 1$ iii) $y = 3 - 4x$ iv) $xy = 6$

(Level 8)

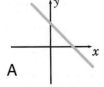

A

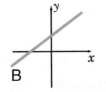

B

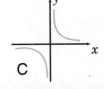

C

D

How well did you do?   ✗ 1–4 Try again   5–10 Getting there   11–15 Good work   16–18 Excellent! ✓

Shapes

Polygons

Polygons are **2D** shapes with straight sides. Regular polygons are shapes with all sides equal and angles equal.

 Try to learn all the shapes and their symmetrical properties.

Number of sides	Name of polygon
3	**Triangle**
4	**Quadrilateral**
5	**Pentagon**
6	**Hexagon**
7	**Heptagon**
8	**Octagon**

Regular pentagon
- five equal sides
- rotational symmetry of order 5
- five lines of symmetry

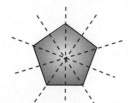

Regular hexagon
- six equal sides
- rotational symmetry of order 6
- six lines of symmetry

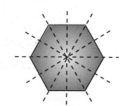

Regular octagon
- eight equal sides
- rotational symmetry of order 8
- eight lines of symmetry

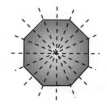

Quadrilaterals

Quadrilaterals are four-sided shapes.

Square
- four lines of symmetry
- rotational symmetry of order 4

Rectangle
- two lines of symmetry
- rotational symmetry of order 2

Parallelogram
- no lines of symmetry
- rotational symmetry of order 2

Rhombus
- two lines of symmetry
- rotational symmetry of order 2

Kite
- one line of symmetry
- no rotational symmetry

Trapezium

Isosceles trapezium
- one line of symmetry
- no rotational symmetry

Scalene trapezium
- no lines of symmetry
- no rotational symmetry

 Parallel lines are always the same distance apart, they never meet.

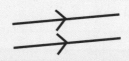

Triangles

There are several types of **triangle**.

 You need to be able to sketch all these shapes and know their symmetrical properties.

Right-angled
- one 90° angle

Equilateral
- three sides equal
- three angles equal

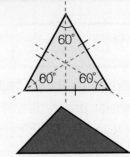

Isosceles
- two sides equal
- base angles equal

Scalene
- no sides or angles the same

The circle

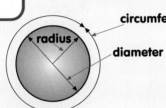

The angle in a semicircle is always a right angle.

- **diameter** = 2 × **radius**

The **circumference** is the distance round the outside edge.

The **perpendicular bisector** of a chord passes through the centre of a circle.

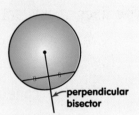

A **chord** is a straight line that joins two points on the circumference.
A chord that passes through the centre is a **diameter**.
A **tangent** touches the circle at one point only.
An **arc** is part of the circumference.

The radius and tangent at a point make an angle of 90°.

KEY TERMS

Make sure you understand these terms before moving on!

- 2D
- arc
- chord
- circumference
- diameter
- equilateral
- heptagon
- hexagon
- isosceles
- kite
- octagon
- parallelogram
- pentagon
- perpendicular bisector
- polygon
- quadrilateral
- radius
- rectangle
- rhombus
- right-angle
- scalene
- square
- triangle
- tangent
- trapezium

QUICK TEST

1. What is the name of a six-sided polygon?
2. From memory, draw all the main triangles and quadrilaterals.

Solids

3D shapes

A prism is a solid that can be cut into slices which are all the same shape.

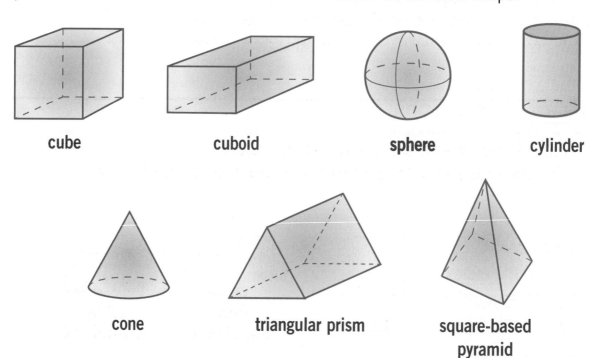

cube   cuboid   **sphere**   cylinder

cone   triangular prism   square-based pyramid

Nets of solids

The **net** of a **3D** shape is the 2D (flat) shape, which is folded to make the 3D shape.

Examples

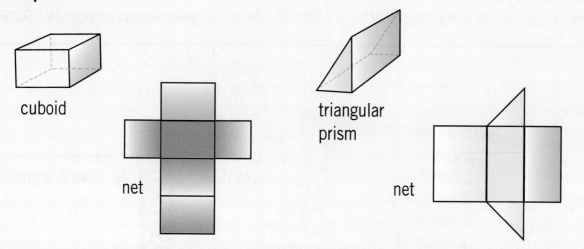

cuboid

net

triangular prism

net

> When making the shape, remember to put tabs on, to stick it together.
>
> When asked to draw an accurate net, you must measure carefully.
>
> When drawing nets accurately, make sure that you are careful when measuring the sides.

Faces, edges and vertices

A **face** is a flat surface of a solid.
An **edge** is where two faces meet.
Vertex is another word for a corner.
The plural is **vertices**.
A cuboid has six faces, eight vertices and 12 edges.
Edges that cannot be seen are usually shown with dotted lines.

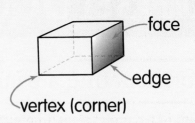

face

edge

vertex (corner)

Plans and elevations

A **plan** is what is seen if a 3D shape is viewed from above.
An **elevation** is what is seen if the 3D shape is viewed from the side or front.

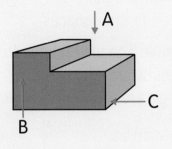

A

B

C

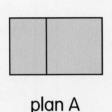

plan A

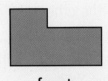

front
elevation B

side
elevation C

QUICK TEST

1. Draw an accurate net of this 3D shape.

5.7 cm

4 cm

4 cm

4 cm

2. Draw a sketch of the plan and elevations of this solid from A and B.

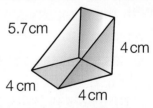
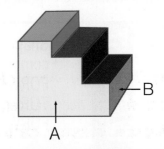

B

A

Constructions & LOGO

Constructing a triangle

Example: Use **compasses** to **construct** this triangle.

- Draw the longest side.
- With the compass point at A, draw an **arc** of radius 4 cm.
- With the compass point at B, draw an arc of radius 5 cm.
- Join A and B to the point where the two arcs meet at C.

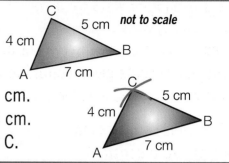

Bisecting an angle

- Draw two lines XY and YZ to meet at an angle.
- Using compasses, place the point at Y and draw two arcs, one on XY and the other on YZ.
- Place the compass point on the two arcs on XY and YZ and draw arcs to cross at N. Join Y to N. YN is the **bisector** of angle XYZ.

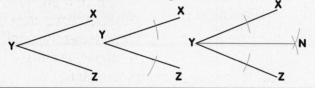

LOGO

- **LOGO** is a computer program used to draw shapes.

Example The instructions to draw an equilateral triangle are:
FORWARD 4
TURN RIGHT 120°
FORWARD 4
TURN RIGHT 120°
FORWARD 4

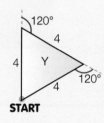

Perpendicular bisector of a line

- Draw a line XY.
- Set the compasses to a radius greater than the distance XY. With the compasses centred on X, draw two arcs as shown.
- With the compasses set at the same radius, draw two arcs centred on Y.
- Join the two points where the arcs cross.
- AB is the **perpendicular bisector** of XY.
- N is the **midpoint** of XY.

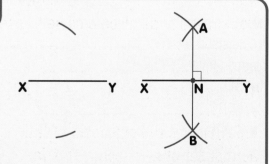

You will need to be able to do these constructions, to answer questions on loci or scale drawings.

QUICK TEST

❶ Shape A is a rectangle. Complete the LOGO commands for drawing the rectangle:
FORWARD 2
TURN RIGHT 90°
FORWARD 5

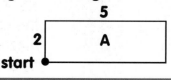

❷ Bisect this angle.

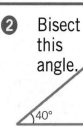

Loci & coordinates in 3D

LOCI & COORDINATES IN 3D Shape, space and measures

Common loci

- The **locus** of a point is the set of all possible positions which that point can occupy, subject to some given condition or rule.
- The plural of locus is loci.

a The locus of the points which are a constant distance from a fixed point is a circle.

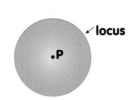
locus
•P

b The locus of the points which are equidistant from two points X and Y is the perpendicular bisector of XY.

perpendicular bisector
X _____ Y

c The locus of the points **equidistant** from two intersesting lines is the line that bisects the angle.

locus

d The locus of the points at a constant distance from a line XY is a pair of **parallel lines**, above and below XY

X————————Y

Example

John wants to plant a rose tree. The tree must be at least 4 metres from the house, and at least 4 metres from the corner A of the greenhouse. Show accurately on the diagram the region in which John can plant his rose tree. (You would usually be given a scale to use.)

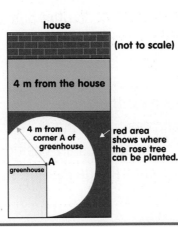
house
(not to scale)
4 m from the house
4 m from corner A of greenhouse
red area shows where the rose tree can be planted.
A
greenhouse

🛈 *Loci must be drawn carefully and measured accurately. When answering 'loci' questions, use the construction techniques previously shown; this will ensure that your work is accurate.*

Coordinates in 3D

This involves the extension of the normal set of x–y coordinates in a third direction, known as z. All positions then have three coordinates (x, y, z).

Example For the cuboid the vertices would have the following coordinates:

A (3, 0, 0)   B (3, 2, 0)
C (0, 2, 0)   D (0, 2, 1)
E (0, 0, 1)   F (3, 0, 1)
G (3, 2, 1)   O (0, 0, 0)

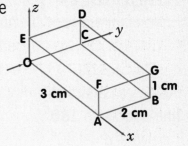
3 cm   1 cm   2 cm

Make sure you understand these terms before moving on!
- equidistant
- locus

QUICK TEST

❶ A gold coin is buried in the rectangular field. It is 4 m from T and equidistant from RU and RS. Mark with an X the position of the gold coin. (Note: draw the diagram with a scale of 1 cm to 1 m to answer this properly.)

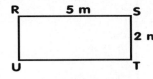
R   5 m   S
2 m
U   T

Angles & tessellations

Angles and the protractor

An angle is an amount of turn or rotation. Angles are measured with a protractor, in degrees. The area surrounding a point can be divided into 360 parts. Each part is called a degree and is represented by a small circle °.

- There are

 An **acute** angle is between 0° and 90°.

 An **obtuse** angle is between 90° and 180°.

 A **reflex** angle is between 180° and 360°.

A **right angle** is 90°.

Measuring angles with a protractor

A **protractor** is used to measure the size of an angle.
For the angle on the right measure on the outer scale since you must start from 0°.
Beware, make sure one arm of the angle is along the base line, and read from the correct scale with the 0° line at the start position.
When measuring angles, count the degree lines carefully and always double check.

Read from 0° on the outer scale.

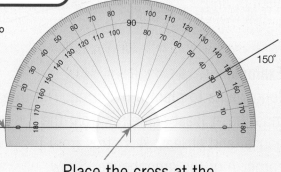

150°

Place the cross at the point of the angle you are measuring.

Angle facts

Angles on a **straight line** add up to **180°**.
$a + b + c = 180°$

Angles at a **point** add up to **360°**.
$a + b + c = 360°$

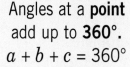

Angles in a **triangle** add up to **180°**
$a + b + c = 180°$

Angles in a **quadrilateral** add up to **360°**.
$a + b + c + d = 360°$

Vertically opposite angles are equal.
$a = b, c = d$
$a + c = b + d = 180°$

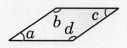

An **exterior** angle of a triangle equals the sum of the two opposite **interior** angles.
$a + b = c$

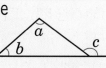

You must remember these angle facts as you will need to apply them to questions.
Two angles that add up to 180° are **supplementary**.

Angles in parallel lines

Alternate (Z) angles are **equal**.

Corresponding angles are **equal**.

Allied or **co-interior** angles are **supplementary**, they add up to **180°**.
$c + d = 180°$

Reading angles

When asked to find ABC or ∠ABC or AB̂C, find the angle shown by the middle letter, in this case B.

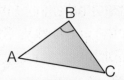

Angles in polygons

There are two types of angles in a polygon: interior (inside) and exterior (outside).

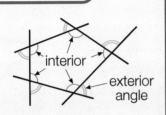

For a regular polygon with n sides:
- sum of exterior angles = 360°
  so exterior angle = $\frac{360°}{n}$
- interior angle + exterior angle = 180°
- sum of interior angles = $(n - 2) × 180°$

Example
Calculate the interior and exterior angle of a regular pentagon.
A pentagon has 5 sides, so $n = 5$.
Exterior angle = $\frac{360}{5} = 72°$
Interior angle + exterior angle = 180°
Interior angle = $180° - 72° = 108°$

Angle questions

Find the angles labelled by letters.

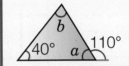

$a + 110° = 180°$
$a = 70°$.
$70° + 40° + b = 180°$
$b = 180° - 110° = 70°$

$a = 70°$ (alternate)
$b = 70°$ (corresponding)
$c = 70°$ (corresponding to a)
$d = 180 - 70 = 110°$ (angles on a straight line)

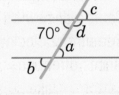

> **Always make sure that you show full working when carrying out an angle calculation.**

KEY TERMS
Make sure you understand these terms before moving on!
- allied
- acute
- alternate
- co-interior
- corresponding
- exterior
- interior
- obtuse
- protractor
- reflex
- right angle
- supplementary
- tessellation
- vertically opposite

Tessellations

- A **tessellation** is a pattern of 2D shapes which fit together without leaving any gaps.
- For shapes to tessellate, the angles at each point must add up to 360°.

Example

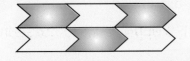

QUICK TEST

❶ Find the size of the angles labelled by letters:

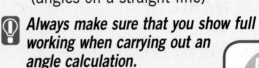
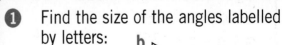

❷ Find the size of **a** an exterior and **b** an interior angle of a regular hexagon

Bearings & scale drawings

Compass points

The diagram shows the points of the **compass**.

Example

If Paulo is facing east and turns clockwise through an angle of 270°, what direction will he now be facing?

Paulo will now be facing North. Remember clockwise is this direction.

Bearings

- **Bearings** give a direction in degrees.
- Bearings are always measured from the north in a **clockwise** direction.
- They must have three figures.

Examples

Bearing of A from B
= 180° − 50° = 130°.

Measure from the North line at B.

Bearing of A from B
= 360° − 30° = 330°.

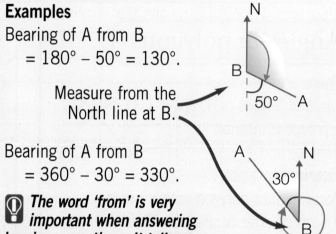

🛈 *The word 'from' is very important when answering bearings questions. It tells you where to put the North line and measure from.*

Back bearings

When finding the **back bearing** (the bearing of B from A below):
- draw a north line at A
- use the properties of parallel lines, since both north lines are parallel.

Examples

Bearing of B from A
= 360° − 50°
= 310°.

Bearing of B from A
= 180° − 30°
= 150°.

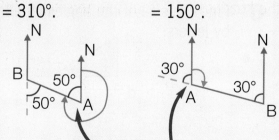

Measure from the north line at A.

Look for alternate (Z) or corresponding angles.

Scale drawings

Scale drawings are very useful for finding lengths that cannot be measured directly.

Example

This is a rough sketch of a **sector** of a circle. Using a scale of 1 cm to 2 m, draw an accurate drawing of the sector.

A scale of 1 cm to 2 m means that 6.8 m is 6.8 ÷ 2 = 3.4 cm on the diagram.

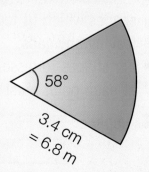

Scales and maps

Scales are often used on maps. They are usually written as a ratio.

Example

Q The scale on a road map is 1 : 25 000. Bury and Oldham are 20 cm apart on the map. Work out the real distance, in km, between Bury and Oldham.

A Scale 1 : 25 000 and distance on map is 20 cm.

Real distance = 20 × 25 000 = 500 000 cm.

Divide by 100 to change cm to m: 500 000 ÷ 100 = 5000 m

Divide by 1000 to change m to km: 5000 ÷ 1000 = 5 km

A scale of 1 : 25 000 means that 1 cm on the scale drawing represents a real length of 25 000 cm.

Scale drawings and bearings

Scale drawings are very useful for finding lengths that cannot be measured directly.

Example

A ship sails from a harbour for 15 km on a bearing of 040°, and then continues due east for 20 km. Make a scale drawing of this journey, using a scale of 1 cm to 5 km. How far will the ship have to sail to get back to the harbour by the shortest route?

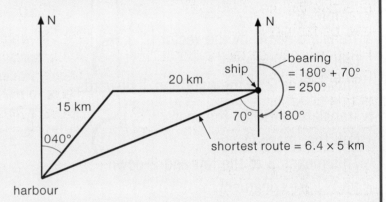

What will the bearing be?

Shortest route = 6.4 × 5 km = 32 km. Bearing = 70° + 180° = 250°.

QUICK TEST

1 What are the bearings of X from Y in the following?

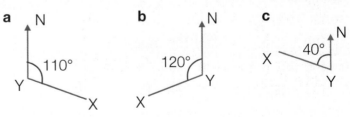

2 For each of the questions above work out the bearings of Y from X.

Transformations

- A *transformation* changes the position or size of a shape.
- The four types of transformation are: translation, reflection, rotation and enlargement.

Translations

- **Translations** move figures from one place to another.
- The original shape is the object and the new shape is the image.
- The size and shape of the figure are not changed.

Vectors are used to describe the distance and direction of the translation.

A vector is written as $\begin{pmatrix} a \\ b \end{pmatrix}$.

a represents the horizontal movement, and
b represents the vertical movement.

Example
a Translate △ABC by the vector $\begin{pmatrix} 2 \\ 1 \end{pmatrix}$.
  Call it the image P.
  This means 2 to the right and 1 upwards.

b Translate △ABC by the vector $\begin{pmatrix} -3 \\ -2 \end{pmatrix}$.
  Call the image Q.
  This means 3 to the left and 2 down.

P and Q are **congruent**.

Remember that two shapes are congruent if one is exactly the same as the other.

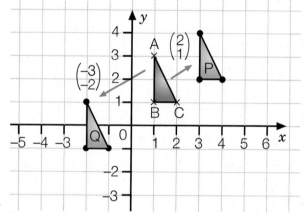

Reflections

Reflections create an image of an object on the other side of a mirror line. The mirror line is known as an **axis of reflection**. The size and shape of the figure are not changed.

Example
Reflect triangle ABC in:
a the x-axis, and call the image D
b the line $y = -x$, and call the image E
c the line $x = 5$, and call the image F.

D, E and F are congruent to triangle ABC.

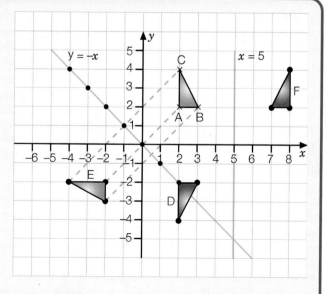

 Count the squares of the object from the mirror. It's easier.

Rotations

Rotations **turn** a figure through an angle about some fixed point.
This fixed point is called the **centre of rotation**.
The size and shape of the figure are not changed.

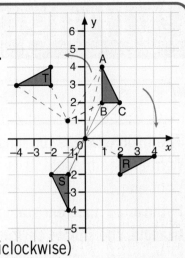

Example Rotate triangle ABC:

a   90° **clockwise** about (0, 0) and call the image R

b   180° about (0, 0), and call the image S

c   90° **anticlockwise** about (–1, 1), and call the image T.

When describing a rotation give: the centre of rotation, the
angle of the turn and the direction of the turn (clockwise or anticlockwise)

Enlargements

- **Enlargements** change the size but not the shape of an object.
- The point from which the enlargement takes place is the **centre of enlargement**.
- The **scale factor** indicates how many times longer each length of the original figure becomes.
- If the scale factor is **greater than 1**, the shape becomes **bigger**.
- If the scale factor is **less than 1**, the shape becomes **smaller**.

Example
Enlarge shape ABCDEF by a scale factor of 2, centre (0, 0). Call the image A′ B′ C′ D′ E′ F′. Notice that each side of the enlargement is twice the length of the original. OA′ = 2 × OA.

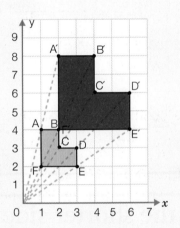

Example
ABC has been enlarged with a scale factor $\frac{1}{2}$, to give A′B′C′. The centre of enlargement is at O.

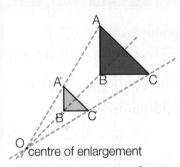

centre of enlargement

Notice that OA′ is $\frac{1}{2}$ OA. If asked to describe an enlargement, state the centre of enlargement and the scale factor.

KEY TERMS

Make sure you understand these terms before moving on!

- axis of reflection
- centre of enlargement
- centre of rotation
- congruent
- enlargement
- reflection
- rotation
- scale factor
- transformation
- translation
- vector

QUICK TEST

❶ Copy the diagram on the right.

a Translate ABC by the vector $\begin{pmatrix} -3 \\ 1 \end{pmatrix}$.
Call the image P.

b Reflect ABC in the line $y = x$. Call the image Q.

c Reflect ABC in the line $y = -1$. Call the image R.

d Rotate ABC 180° about (0, 0). Call the image S.

Pythagoras' theorem

Definition of Pythagoras' theorem

The **hypotenuse** is the longest side of a right-angled triangle. It is always opposite the right angle.

Pythagoras' theorem states: in any **right-angled triangle**, the **square** on the hypotenuse is equal to the sum of the squares on the other two sides. Pythagoras' theorem allows you to calculate the length of any side in a right-angled triangle, provided the lengths of the other two sides are known.

Using the letters in the diagram the theorem is written as:

$$c^2 = a^2 + b^2$$

This may be rearranged to give:

$$b^2 = c^2 - a^2$$
$$a^2 = c^2 - b^2$$

Use these when calculating shorter sides.

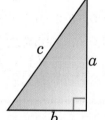

Finding the hypotenuse

Example

Find the length of XY, giving your answer to 1 d.p. Using Pythagoras' theorem gives:

$$XY^2 = XZ^2 + ZY^2$$
$$= 10^2 + 12.5^2$$
$$XY^2 = 256.25$$
$$XY = \sqrt{256.25}$$
$$= 16.0 \text{ m (1 dp)}$$

Take the **square root** to find XY

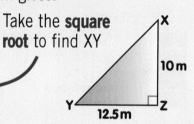

Example

Calculate the value of x. Give your answer to 2 dp.

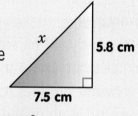

$$x^2 = 7.5^2 + 5.8^2$$
$$= 56.25 + 33.64$$
$$= 89.89$$
$$x = \sqrt{89.89}$$
$$x = 9.48 \text{ cm (2 dp)}$$

Finding the length of the shorter side

Rearrange the formula and use $a^2 = c^2 - b^2$.

Example

Find the length of CD, giving your answer to 1 dp. Using Pythagoras' Theorem gives:

$$CE^2 = CD^2 + DE^2$$
$$CD^2 = CE^2 - DE^2$$
$$CD^2 = 12^2 - 4.2^2$$
$$CD^2 = \sqrt{126.36}$$
$$CD = \sqrt{126.36}$$
$$CD = 11.2 \text{ m (1 d.p.)}$$

Example

Find the length of y in the triangle. Give your answer to 3 sf.

$$15^2 = y^2 + 6.9^2$$
$$15^2 - 6.9^2 = y^2$$
$$255 - 47.61 = y^2$$
$$177.39 = y^2$$
$$y = \sqrt{177.39}$$
$$y = 13.3 \text{ m (3 sf)}$$

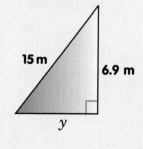

Calculating the distance between two coordinates

By drawing in a triangle between the two points A (1, 2) and B (7, 6) we can find the length of AB by Pythagoras' theorem using the **coordinates**.

Horizontal distance = $7 - 1 = 6$
Vertical distance = $6 - 2 = 4$

Length of $(AB)^2 = 6^2 + 4^2$
$(AB)^2 = 36 + 16$
$(AB)^2 = 52$
$(AB)^2 = \sqrt{52}$

Length of AB = 7.21
The **midpoint** of AB, M has coordinates
(4, 4) i.e. $\left(\dfrac{1+7}{2}, \dfrac{2+6}{2}\right)$

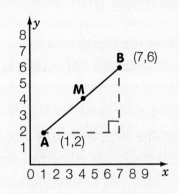

Problems

Pythagoras' Theorem can be used to solve practical problems.

Example

Seagull Point is 12.5 km West and 6.7 km North of Fisherman's Cove. Calculate the direct distance from Seagull Point to Fisherman's Cove. Call the distance between Seagull Point and Fisherman's Cove x.

$x^2 = 12.5^2 + 6.7^2$

$x^2 = 201.14$

$x = \sqrt{201.14}$

$x = 14.2$ km (1 d.p.)

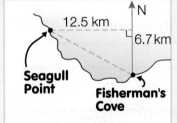

Seagull Point · Fisherman's Cove

Make sure you understand these terms before moving on!
- coordinates
- hypotenuse
- Pythagoras' theorem
- right-angled triangle
- square
- square root

1 Calculate the length of each side marked with a letter. Give your answers to 1 dp. **c**

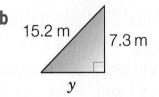

a
12 m
x
6.9 m

b
15.2 m
7.3 m
y

2 A ship sets off from Port A and travels 50 km north then 80 km East to reach Port B. How far is Port A from Port B, by the shortest route? **c**

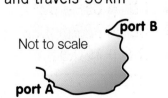

Not to scale

port B
port A

Trigonometry

Trigonometry in right-angled triangles can be used to calculate an unknown angle or an unknown length (Level 8).

Labelling the sides of the triangle

The **hypotenuse (hyp)** is opposite the right angle.
The **opposite** side **(opp)** is opposite the angle θ.
The **adjacent** side **(adj)** is next to the angle θ.
θ is a greek letter called **theta** and is used to represent **angles**.

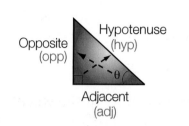

Trigonometric ratios

The three **trigonometric ratios** are:

$$\text{sine (sin) } \theta = \frac{\text{opposite}}{\text{hypotenuse}} \qquad \text{cosine (cos) } \theta = \frac{\text{adjacent}}{\text{hypotenuse}} \qquad \text{tangent (tan) } \theta = \frac{\text{opposite}}{\text{adjacent}}$$

The made-up word **SOH CAH TOA** is a quick way of remembering the ratios. The word comes from the first letters of **s**in equals **o**pposite divided by **h**ypotenuse, and so on.

To enter sin 30° into the calculator you may need to do it backwards, as [3] [0] [sin] although some calculators do it forwards: check yours!

Calculating the size of an angle

Example
Calculate angle ABC.

$\tan \theta = \dfrac{\text{opp}}{\text{adj}}$ Label the sides and decide on the ratio.

$\tan \theta = \dfrac{15}{27}$ Divide the top value by the bottom value.

$\tan \theta = 0.\dot{5}$ ←
$\quad \theta = 29.1°$ (1 dp)

It is important not to round here. Keep as 0.$\dot{5}$ not 0.6.

On the calculator key in

[1] [5] [÷] [2] [7] [=] [INV] [tan] [=]

You may have a shift key on your calculator.
To find the angle you usually use the second function on your calculator.

Check your calculator as you may have to do it differently.

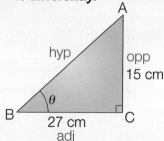

Calculating the length of a side

Example
Calculate the length of BC.
- Label the sides first.

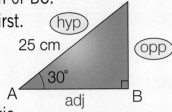

- Decide on the ratio.

$$\sin 30° = \frac{\text{opp}}{\text{hyp}}$$

- Substitute in the values.

$$\sin 30° = \frac{BC}{25}$$

$25 \times \sin 30° = BC$ Multiply both sides by 25.

$BC = 12.5$ cm

Example
Calculate the length of EF.

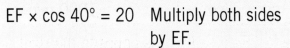

$$\cos 40° = \frac{\text{adj}}{\text{hyp}} = \frac{20}{EF}$$

$EF \times \cos 40° = 20$ Multiply both sides by EF.

$$EF = \frac{20}{\cos 40°}$$ Divide both sides by $\cos 40°$.

$= 26.1$ cm (1 dp)

| 2 | 0 | ÷ | 4 | 0 | cos | = |

or

| 2 | 0 | ÷ | cos | 4 | 0 | = |

💡 *The size of an angle should usually be rounded to 1 dp. However do not round your answer until right at the end of the question. You need to learn the trigonometric ratios.*

KEY TERMS
Make sure you understand these terms before moving on!
- adjacent side
- angle of depression
- angle of elevation
- cosine
- hypotenuse
- opposite side
- ratio
- sine
- tangent
- theta
- trigonometry

Angles of elevation and depression

The **angle of elevation** is measured from the horizontal **upwards**.

The **angle of depression** is measured from the horizontal **downwards**.

QUICK TEST

1 Calculate the length of x in each triangle. **c**

a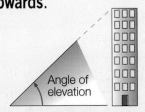

b c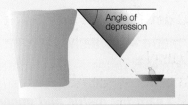

2 Work out the size of the angle θ in each of these triangles. **c**

a

b c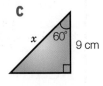

3 a Calculate the length of BN.
   b Calculate the length of BC.
   c Calculate the size of ∠BCN.

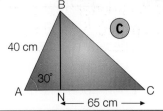

Measures & measurement 1

Metric units

Length
10 mm = 1 cm
100 cm = 1 m
1000 m = 1 km

Weight
1000 mg = 1 **gram**
1000 g = 1 kg
1000 kg = 1 tonne

Capacity
1000 ml = 1 **litre**
100 cl = 1 litre
1000 cm³ = 1 litre

Converting units
- If changing from **small** units to **large** units (e.g. g to kg) **divide**.
- If changing from **large** units to **small** units (e.g. km to m) **multiply**.

Examples 500 cm = 5 **metres** (÷ 100)   5 litres = 500 cl (× 100)
3500 g = 3.5 kg (÷ 1000)   25 cm = 250 mm (× 10)

 Try to remember these metric equivalents.

Imperial units

Length
12 **inches** = 1 **foot**
3 feet = 1 **yard**

Weight
16 **ounces** (oz) = 1 **pound**
14 pounds (lb) = 1 **stone**

Capacity
20 **fluid oz** = 1 **pint**
8 pints = 1 **gallon**

Comparisons between metric and imperial units

Length
2.5 cm ≈ 1 inch
30 cm ≈ 1 foot
1 metre ≈ 39 inches
8 km ≈ 5 miles

Weight
25 g ≈ 1 ounce
1 kg ≈ 2.2 pounds

Capacity
1 litre ≈ $1\frac{3}{4}$ pints
4.5 litres ≈ 1 gallon

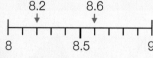 *Learn the metric and imperial conversions. To help you remember them, try learning with a friend and testing each other.*

Example Change 8 inches into cm
1 inch ≈ 2.5 cm
8 inches ≈ 8 × 2.5 = 20 cm
Check to see if your answer sounds sensible.

Reading scales

Decimals are usually used when reading scales. Measuring jugs, rulers and weighing scales are all examples of scales that have decimals.

Examples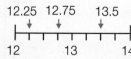

There are 10 spaces between the 8 and the 9. Each space is 0.1.

There are five spaces between the 6 and the 7. Each space is 0.2.

There are four spaces between the 12 and 13. Each space is 0.25.

Accuracy of measurement

Continuous measurements

- **Continuous measurements** are made by using a measuring instrument, for example, the height of a person.
- Continuous measures are not exact.

Example

Lucy is 167 cm tall, correct to the nearest cm. Her actual height could be anywhere between 166.5 cm and 167.5 cm.

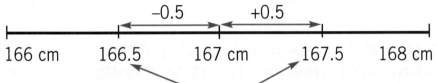

These two values are the limits of Lucy's height.

If *H* represents height, then $166.5 \leqslant H < 167.5$

This is the **lower limit** of Lucy's height. Anything over 166.5 but below 167.5 is recorded as 167 cm.

Remember that these measurements cannot be **equal** to the upper limit.

This is the **upper limit** of Lucy's height. Anything from 166.5 up to 167.5 would be recorded as 167 cm.

 In general, if a measurement is accurate to some given amount, then the true value lies within a maximum of a half a unit of that amount.

QUICK TEST

1. Change 6 200 g into kg.
2. Change 4.2 cm into mm.
3. Change 6 litres into pints.
4. What do the pointers on the scales represent?

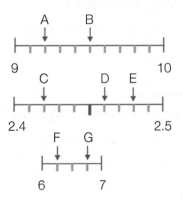

5. Write down the upper and lower limits for a time of 6.3 seconds, rounded to the nearest tenth of a second.

Measures & Measurement 2

Compound measures

Speed can be measured in kilometres per hour (km/h), miles per hour (m.p.h.) and metres per second (m/s). These are all **compound measures**, because they involve a combination of basic measures – in this case, **distance** and **time**.

Speed

average speed = $\dfrac{\text{total distance travelled}}{\text{total time taken}} = \dfrac{D}{T}$ time = $\dfrac{\text{distance}}{\text{speed}}$ distance = speed × time

Use this triangle to help you remember the formulae. $\dfrac{D}{S \times T}$

Example Lynette walks 10 km in 4 hours. Find her average speed.

$S = \dfrac{D}{T} = \dfrac{10}{4} = 2.5$ km/h

Example Sam travels at a speed of 60 km/h. If he travels 250 km, how long does the journey take?

$T = \dfrac{D}{S} = \dfrac{250}{60} = 4.1\dot{6}$ hours = 4 hours 10 minutes

To find the minutes multiply $0.1\dot{6}$ by 60.

Density

density = $\dfrac{\text{mass}}{\text{volume}} = \dfrac{M}{V}$ volume = $\dfrac{\text{mass}}{\text{density}} = \dfrac{M}{D}$ mass = density × volume = $D \times V$

Since the mass is in grams and the volume in cubic centimetres (cm^3), density is in g/cm^3. Use this triangle to help you remember the formulae. $\dfrac{M}{D \times V}$

Example

Find the density of an object of mass 600 g and volume 50 cm^3.

Density = $\dfrac{M}{V} = \dfrac{600}{50} = 12$ g/cm^3.

Just remember the letters – it is quicker.

Before starting a question always check the units and change them if necessary.

QUICK TEST

1. It takes Bina 30 minutes to walk to the shop 2 km away. At what speed is she travelling?

2. The mass of an object is 500 grams. If the density is 6.2 g/cm^3 what is the volume of the object? **C**

3. Bonnie travels to work at a speed of 40 mph. If she works 30 miles away, how long will it take her to get to work? **C**

KEY TERMS
Make sure you understand these terms before moving on!
■ compound measure
■ density ■ distance
■ mass ■ speed
■ time ■ volume

68

Similar shapes Level 8

Similar figures are the **same shape** but **different sizes**.
Corresponding angles are **equal**.
Corresponding lengths are in the same **ratio**.
Congruent shapes are exactly the same shape and size.

Examples
Corresponding angles are equal.

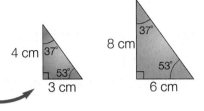

Corresponding lengths are in the same ratio. The lengths on the bigger cone are twice those in the smaller cone.

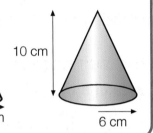

Finding missing lengths of similar figures

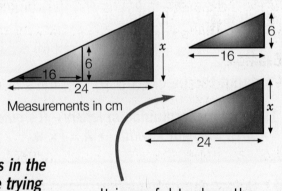

Example Find the missing length a, giving your answer to 2 sf.

$\frac{a}{11} = \frac{9}{14}$ Corresponding sides are in the same ratio.

$a = \frac{9}{14} \times 11$ Multiply both sides by 11.

$a = 7.1$ cm (2 sf)

Example Calculate the missing length.

$\frac{x}{6} = \frac{24}{16}$ Corresponding sides are in the same ratio.

$x = \frac{24}{16} \times 6$ Multiply both sides by 6.

$x = 9$ cm

Measurements in cm

💡 *Always make sure you put the corresponding sides in the correct order and remember that whatever you are trying to work out must go on the top of the fraction otherwise you will have a tricky calculation to do.*

It is useful to draw the two triangles first.

KEY TERMS

Make sure you understand these terms before moving on!
- congruent
- corresponding
- ratio
- similar

QUICK TEST

❶ Find the lengths labelled by the letters in these similar shapes.

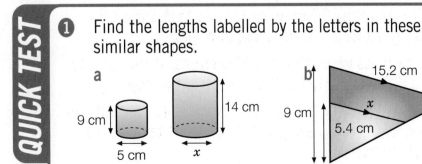

a

b

2D shapes

Perimeter is the distance around the outside edge of a shape.

Area is the amount of space a 2D shape covers. Common units of area are square millimetres (mm^2), square centimetres (cm^2), and square metres (m^2).

Areas of quadrilaterals and triangles

Area of a rectangle

Area = length × width

$A = l \times w$

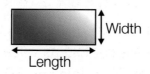
Width
Length

Area of a triangle

$A = \frac{1}{2}$ × base × **perpendicular height**

$A = \frac{1}{2} \times b \times h$

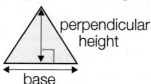
perpendicular height
base

Area of a trapezium

$A = \frac{1}{2}$ × (sum of parallel sides)
× **perpendicular distance**
between sides

Perpendicular height just means the height, which is at 90° to the base.

$A = \frac{1}{2} \times (a + b) \times h$

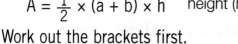
height (h)
a
b

Work out the brackets first.

> 💡 *Write the formuulae in letters – it's quicker.*
> *Area = length × width → A = l × w.*

Area of a parallelogram

Area = base × perpendicular height

$A = b \times h$

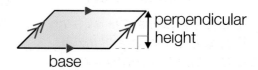
perpendicular height
base

Examples
Find the area of these shapes.

a

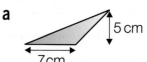
5 cm
7 cm

$A = \frac{1}{2} \times b \times h$

$A = \frac{1}{2} \times 7 \times 5 = 17.5 \ cm^2$

b

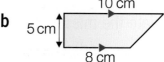
10 cm
5 cm
8 cm

$A = \frac{1}{2} \times (a + b) \times h$

$A = \frac{1}{2} \times (10 + 8) \times 5 = 45 \ cm^2$

Circumference and area of a circle 1

Circumference = π × diameter   Area = π × (radius)²

$C = \pi \times d$ $A = \pi \times r^2$

$= 2 \times \pi \times radius$

$= 2 \times \pi \times r$

radius
diameter
circumference

Example Find the circumference and area of this circle (Use π = 3.14):

$C = \pi \times d$ $A = \pi \times r^2$ $(r = 10 \div 2 = 5)$

$= 3.14 \times 10$ $A = 3.14 \times 5^2$

$= 31.4 \ cm$ $= 78.5 \ cm^2$

10 cm

Circumference and area of a circle 2

Example

Find the area of a circular rose garden with a diameter of 2.6 metres. Use $\pi = 3.142$.

Diameter = 2.6 m

Radius = 2.6 ÷ 2 = 1.3 m

Area = $\pi \times r^2$

Remember r^2 means $r \times r$.

= 3.142×1.3^2

Remember 1.3^2 means 1.3×1.3

= 5.3 m² (1 dp)

💡 *Always check that the units are the same before beginning a question on area or perimeter. Check that you have written the units for your answer as you may be awarded marks for this.*

Example

Mohammed's bicycle wheel has a diameter of 60 cm. Work out the circumference of the wheel, using $\pi = 3.14$. If Mohammed travels a distance of 50 metres on the bicycle, how many times does his wheel turn around?

Remember that the circumference of a circle is the distance around the outside edge.

$$C = \pi \times d = 3.14 \times 60 = 188.4 \text{ cm}$$

Use $\pi = 3.14$ or the value of π on your calculator, if you are not told its value in the question.

Change 50 m into cm: $50 \times 100 = 5000$ cm

Then distance ÷ circumference = number of turns.

$$\frac{5000}{188.4} = 26.5 \text{ turns}$$

The wheel must turn 27 times to cover 50 metres. Check that the answer is sensible.

Areas of enlargements and changing area units

If a shape is enlarged by a scale factor n then the area of the **enlargement** is n^2 times as big as the area of the original.

Example

If $n = 2$:

$A = 1 \text{ cm}^2$

1 cm

$n = 2$

$A = 4 \text{ cm}^2$

2 cm

- the lengths are twice as big
- the area is four times as big ($n^2 = 4$).

Example

The square has a length of 1 metre. This is the same as a length of 100 cm.

Area = 1 m²   Area = 10 000 cm²

Therefore **1 m² = 10 000 cm²**

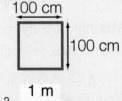

100 cm

100 cm

1 m

1 m

💡 *It is always better to change the units before you start a question.*

KEY TERMS

Make sure you understand these terms before moving on!

- area
- circumference
- enlargement
- perimeter
- perpendicular distance
- perpendicular height

QUICK TEST

❶ Work out the areas of a-d, giving your answers to 1 dp.

a 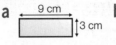 9 cm, 3 cm

b 6 cm, 12 cm

c 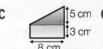 5 cm, 3 cm, 8 cm

d 5 cm

❷ Work out the circumference of a circle with a radius of 4.9 cm. Use $\pi = 3.14$.

❸ Change 40 000 cm² into m².

❹ The area of a shape is 3 cm². If the lengths are enlarged by a scale factor of 3 what is the area of the enlarged shape?

Volume of 3D solids

Calculating volumes of 3D solids

Volume

Volume is the amount of space a **3D** solid occupies. Common units of volume are cubic millimetres (mm^3), cubic centimetres (cm^3) and cubic metres (m^3).

Volume of a cuboid

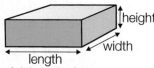

Volume = length × width × height
$$V = l \times w \times h$$

Volume of a prism

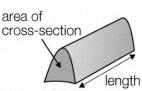

area of cross-section

Volume = area of **cross-section** × length
$$V = a \times l$$

A prism is any solid that can be cut into slices that are all the same shape. This shape is the **uniform cross-section**.

Volume of a cylinder

Volume = area of cross-section × length
$$V = \pi r^2 \times h$$

Area of circle — Height or length

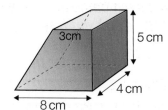

radius

height

Remember, to find the volume of a prism, multiply the area of cross-section by the length.

Example

Dog food is sold in cylindrical tins. Work out the volume of dog food the tin contains. Use $\pi = 3.14$.

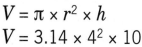

8 cm

DOGGO'S 10cm

Diameter = 8 cm
so Radius = 4 cm
$$V = \pi \times r^2 \times h$$
$$V = 3.14 \times 4^2 \times 10$$
$$V = 502.4 \ cm^3$$

Example

A door wedge is in the shape of a trapezium.
Work out the volume of the door wedge.

3cm   5 cm

4 cm

8 cm

Area of cross-section:

$$A = \tfrac{1}{2}(a + b) \times h$$

$$A = \tfrac{1}{2} \times (3 + 8) \times 5 \ cm^2$$

Volume = $27.5 \times 4 = 110 \ cm^3$

Substitute values in carefully and show full working out.

 For any volume question, work the answer out carefully, check that you show full working and show each step.

Volumes of enlargements

Just like enlarged areas these usually catch people out! For an **enlargement** of scale factor n the volume of the enlarged shape is n^3 times as big as the volume of the original shape.

Example

If a cube of length 1 cm is enlarged by a scale factor of 2 then $n = 2$ so $V = 2^3 = 8$ times bigger.

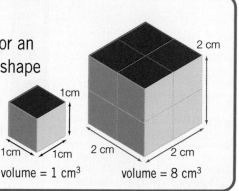

1cm

1cm   1cm

volume = 1 cm^3

2 cm

2 cm   2 cm

volume = 8 cm^3

Converting volume units

Another tricky topic which usually catches everybody out! Change all the lengths to the same unit before starting a question!

Example
The cube has a length of 1 m. This is the same as a length of 100 cm.
Therefore $1 m^3 = 1\,000\,000 cm^3$
not quite what you may think!

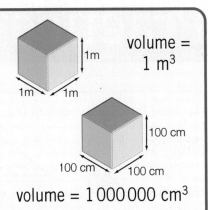

volume = 1 m³

100 cm

volume = 1 000 000 cm³

Dimensions Level 8

- The **dimension** of perimeter is length (L); it is a measurement in one dimension.
- The dimension of area is length × length ($L \times L = L^2$); it is a measurement in two dimensions.

- The dimension of volume is length × length × length ($L \times L \times L = L^3$); it is a measurement in three dimensions.
- Values such as 3, $\frac{4}{\pi}$, 6.2, have no dimensions.

Examples The letters a, b, c and d all represent lengths. For each formula, write down whether it represents a length, area or volume.

a $a^2 + b^2$ = (length × length) + (length × length) = area $L^2 + L^2$

b $\frac{1}{3}\pi abc$ = number × length × length × length = volume L^3

c $2\pi a + \frac{3}{4}\pi d$ = (number × length) + (number × length) = length $L + L$

d $\frac{5}{9}\pi a^2 d + \pi b^2 c^2$ = (number × length × length × length) $L^3 + L^4$
                + (number × length² × length²) = none of the above

This cannot be a length, area or volume formula.   A formula with a mixed dimension is impossible.   A dimension greater than 3 is impossible.

QUICK TEST

① Work out the volume of these 3D shapes, giving your answers to 1 dp. **c**

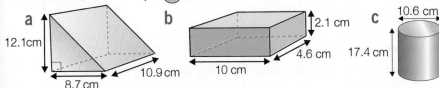

a   12.1cm   8.7 cm
b   2.1 cm   4.6 cm   10.9 cm   10 cm
c   10.6 cm   17.4 cm

② A cuboid has a volume of 6 cm³. If the cuboid is enlarged by a scale factor of 2, calculate the volume of the enlarged solid.

③ x, y, z represent lengths. For each expression, write down whether it could represent perimeter, area or volume.

a $\sqrt{x^2 + y^2 + z^2}$ b $\frac{5}{9}\pi x^3 + 2y^3$

c $\frac{xyz^2}{3y}$ d $\frac{9}{5}\pi xy + \frac{4}{5}\pi yz$

Practice questions

Use the questions to test your progress. Check your answers on page 95.

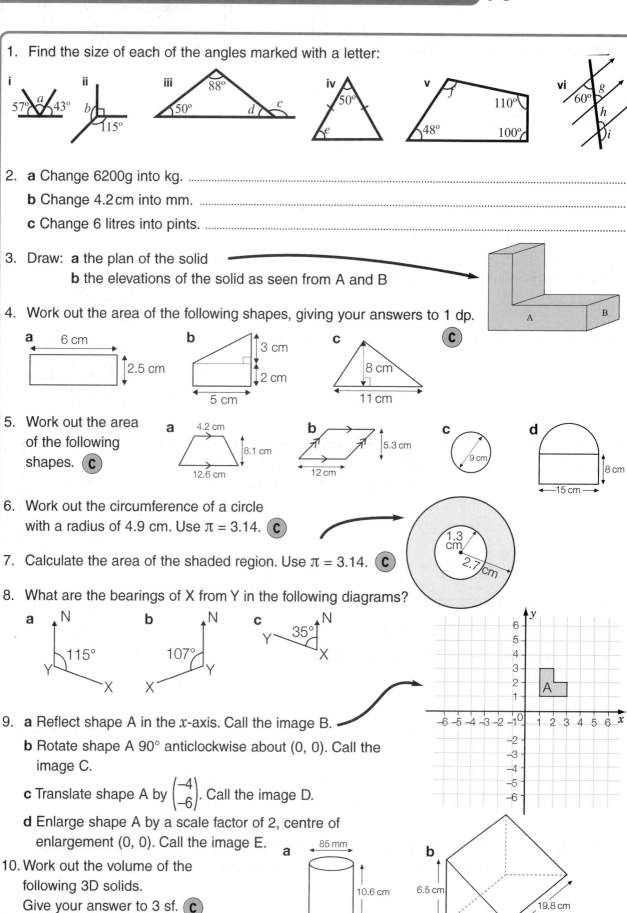

1. Find the size of each of the angles marked with a letter:

   i 57° a 43°

   ii b 115°

   iii 88° 50° d c

   iv 50° e

   v f 110° 48° 100°

   vi 60° g h i

2. **a** Change 6200g into kg. ....

   b Change 4.2cm into mm. ....

   c Change 6 litres into pints. ....

3. Draw: **a** the plan of the solid

   b the elevations of the solid as seen from A and B

4. Work out the area of the following shapes, giving your answers to 1 dp. **C**

   a 6 cm, 2.5 cm

   b 3 cm, 2 cm, 5 cm

   c 8 cm, 11 cm

5. Work out the area of the following shapes. **C**

   a 4.2 cm, 8.1 cm, 12.6 cm

   b 5.3 cm, 12 cm

   c 9 cm

   d 8 cm, 15 cm

6. Work out the circumference of a circle with a radius of 4.9 cm. Use $\pi = 3.14$. **C**

7. Calculate the area of the shaded region. Use $\pi = 3.14$. **C**

   1.3 cm, 2.7 cm

8. What are the bearings of X from Y in the following diagrams?

   a N 115° Y X

   b N 107° Y X

   c N 35° Y X

9. **a** Reflect shape A in the x-axis. Call the image B.

   b Rotate shape A 90° anticlockwise about (0, 0). Call the image C.

   c Translate shape A by $\begin{pmatrix} -4 \\ -6 \end{pmatrix}$. Call the image D.

   d Enlarge shape A by a scale factor of 2, centre of enlargement (0, 0). Call the image E.

10. Work out the volume of the following 3D solids. Give your answer to 3 sf. **C**

    a 85 mm, 10.6 cm

    b 6.5 cm, 27.2 cm, 19.8 cm

11. Calculate the lengths of the sides marked with letters. **a** **b**
    Give your answers to 1 dp. **C**

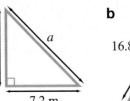 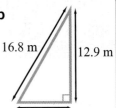

12. Calculate the area of this triangle: **C**

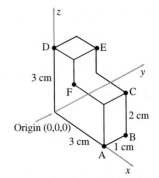

13. Change 7 m² into cm².

....

14. If the volume of a cuboid is 7 m³, work out the volume of the new cuboid if the lengths are
    enlarged by a scale factor of 2.

....

15. Write down the upper and lower limits for a time of 9.2 seconds,
    rounded to the nearest tenth of a second.

....

16. Write down the 3D coordinates for each letter on the solid.

....

....

....

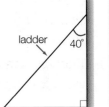

17. (Level 8) A ladder of length 12 m rests against a wall. The angle that the
    ladder makes with the wall is 40°. Calculate the height of the top of the
    ladder above the ground, giving your answer to 1 decimal place. **C**

....

....

18. (Level 8) In the diagram MN is parallel to YZ, YMX and ZNX
    are straight lines, XM = 5.1 cm, XY = 9.5 cm, XN = 6.3 cm,
    YZ = 6.8 cm. ∠YXZ = 29°, ∠XZY = 68°. **C**

    a) i) Calculate the size of angle XMN. ....

       ii) Explain how you obtained your answer. ....

    b) Calculate the length of MN. ....

    c) Calculate the length of XZ. ....

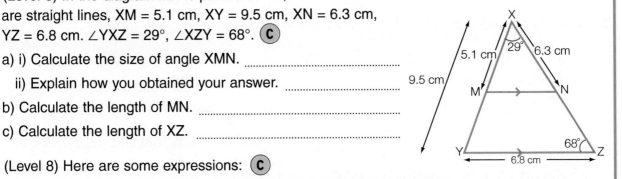

19. (Level 8) Here are some expressions: **C**

$7r^2t$	$v\sqrt{r^2 + t^2}$	$\dfrac{rtv}{4}$	πr^2	$2\sqrt{r^2 + t^2}$	$2tv$	$4\dfrac{r^3}{t^2}$

The letters, r, t and v represent lengths. π, 2, 4 and 7 are numbers that have no dimensions.
Three of the expressions represent surface area. Tick the boxes (✔) underneath these three
expressions.

Collecting data

Types of data

- **Discrete data** – can only take particular values, often found by counting. Examples include the number of red cars in a car park.
- **Continuous data** – can take any value in a given range, often found by measuring. Examples include the heights and weights of year 8 pupils.
- **Primary data** – data that you collect yourself.
- **Secondary data** – data that somebody else has collected (e.g. census).

Collecting information

- Data can be collected by means of a table called a **tally chart** or **frequency table**.
- The tally chart shows the frequency of each item (how often the item occurs).
- A tally is just a line l. Tallies grouped into fives are easier to count. The fifth tally forms a gate, like this ⊮.

Grouping data

If the data includes a large range of results, group the data into **class intervals**, where each class interval is the same width. For continuous data the class intervals are often written using inequalities. Cross off the data as you put it in the table so you do not enter the same item twice.

Example

The heights in cm of 30 pupils were:

137	142	139	120	152	126
149	147	138	135	135	132
127	154	150	138	144	149
150	122	140	142	138	141
149	127	125	141	140	135

Put the data into a tally chart.

- The data has been grouped into class intervals of 5.
- Choose sensible groupings of 2, 5 or 10.
- Check that all data has been included.

Height (h cm)	Tally	Frequency
$120 \leqslant h < 125$	II	2
$125 \leqslant h < 130$	IIII	4
$130 \leqslant h < 135$	I	1
$135 \leqslant h < 140$	⊮ III	8
$140 \leqslant h < 145$	⊮ II	7
$145 \leqslant h < 150$	IIII	4
$150 \leqslant h < 155$	IIII	4
	Total	30

$120 \leqslant h < 125$ means that the heights are all between 120 and 125 cm.

$120 \leqslant h$ means that the height can be equal to 120 cm.

$h < 125$ means that the height cannot be equal to 125 cm. A height of 125 cm would be in the next group.

Always check the total at the end to make sure all data is included.

Stem-and-leaf diagrams

Stem-and-leaf diagrams are used to collect and illustrate information.

Example The heights in cm of some students are:

154, 172, 160, 164, 168, 177, 181, 140, 142, 153, 154, 153, 162

Put into a stem-and-leaf diagram, the information would look like this.

14	0	2		
15	3	3	4	4
16	0	2	4	8
17	2	7		
18	1			

Stem = 10 cm
(Key 18|1 means 181 cm)

For the value 142 cm the stem is 14 and the leaf is 2. This shows that to read off the values you have to multiply the 'stem' by 10 and add on the 'leaf'.

In a stem-and-leaf diagram, all the individual values are recorded. You can read them off the diagram. To make the information easier to read, write the leaves in order.

Surveys and questionnaires

- Data can be collected by carrying out **surveys** using **questionnaires**.
- A **hypothesis** is a prediction that can be tested and usually gives a purpose to the survey, e.g. 'Most staff at the school have red cars'.
- An **observation sheet** is used to collect data. It must be clear and easy to use.

Questionnaires

When designing questionnaires:

- Keep the questionnaire short.
- Give instructions on how to fill it in.
- Ask questions that cover the survey's purpose.
- Do not ask for unnecessary information, e.g. name.
- Word you questions very carefully.
- Make sure that your opinion is not evident, e.g. 'Do you agree that *Neighbours* is better than *Home and Away*?'
- Allow for all possible outcomes.

Example of an observation sheet

Colour of staff cars		
Colour	Tally	Frequency
red		
blue		
white		
green		
black		
others		

Example

How much do you spend on magazines each week?

Under £1 ☐   £1–£1.99 ☐
£2–£2.99 ☐   £3 or over ☐

 When asked to write a questionnaire always word your questions very carefully. Tick boxes are useful when sorting your information.

KEY TERMS

Make sure you understand these terms before moving on!

- class interval
- continuous data
- discrete data
- frequency table
- hypothesis
- observation sheet
- primary data
- questionnaire
- secondary data
- stem-and-leaf diagram
- survey
- tally chart

QUICK TEST

1. Richard and Tammy are carrying out a survey about some students' favourite foods. Design a data collection sheet that they could use.

2. Using a stem of 10, draw a stem-and-leaf diagram for this data: 206, 241, 243, 237, 239, 231, 246, 222, 215, 214, 209, 213, 227

Representing information

Data can be shown in several ways, using different types of diagrams.

Pie charts

Pie charts are circles split up into sections. Each section represents a certain group of items or **category**.

Calculating angles for a pie chart
- Find the total of the data items listed.
- Find the fraction of the total for each data item.
- Multiply the fraction by 360° to find the angle for each category.

> *Remember there are 360° at the centre of the circle. Check that your angles add up to 360°.*

Interpreting pie charts
The pie chart shows how some students travel to school. There are 18 students in total.
How many travel by:
a car? **b** bus? **c** foot?

360° represents 18 students

$1° = \dfrac{18}{360°} = 0.05$ ← Work out what 1° represents

Car: 60° × 0.05 = 3 students
Bus: 80° × 0.05 = 4 students
Walk: 220° × 0.05 = 11 students

Measure the angles carefully with a **protractor**.

Example
These are the favourite sports of 24 students in year 9.

Sport	Frequency
Football	9
Swimming	5
Netball	3
Hockey	7

Finding the angle
9 out of 24 like football,

Multiply by 360°.

$\dfrac{9}{24} × 360° = 135°$

Key in on the calculator:

9 ÷ 2 4 × 3 6 0 =

Football: $\dfrac{9}{24}$ × 360°   = 135°

Swimming: $\dfrac{5}{24}$ × 360°   = 75°

Netball: $\dfrac{3}{24}$ × 360°   = 45°

Hockey: $\dfrac{7}{24}$ × 360°   = 105°

Total = 360°

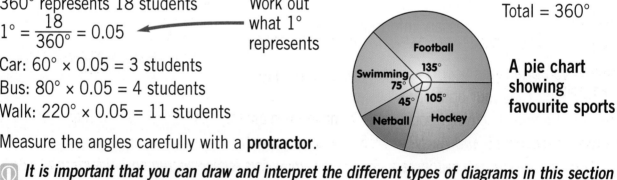

A pie chart showing favourite sports

> *It is important that you can draw and interpret the different types of diagrams in this section as they commonly appear on SATS papers.*

Frequency diagrams 1

- **Frequency diagrams** are drawn to illustrate continuous data.
- There are no gaps between the **bars**.
- The data must be grouped into equal **class intervals** if the height of the bar is used to represent the frequency.
- Check that you've labelled the axes and written a title.

Frequency diagrams 2

Example The heights of 30 pupils are grouped as shown in the table.

- The axes do not always need to start at zero.
- Do not leave gaps between the bars.
- Label the axes and write a title.

Height (h cm)	Frequency
$120 \leqslant h < 125$	2
$125 \leqslant h < 130$	4
$130 \leqslant h < 135$	1
$135 \leqslant h < 140$	8
$140 \leqslant h < 145$	7
$145 \leqslant h < 150$	4
$150 \leqslant h < 155$	4
	30

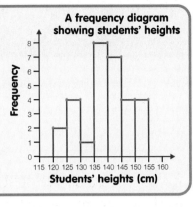

A frequency diagram showing students' heights

Frequency polygons

- To draw a **frequency polygon**, join the **midpoints** of the tops of the bars for the class intervals for grouped or continuous data.
- Put a cross on the middle of each bar and join the crosses with a ruler.
- Draw a line down from the middle of the first and last bars to the x–axis.

Example Consider the bar chart of the students' height. A frequency polygon shows the **trend** of the data.

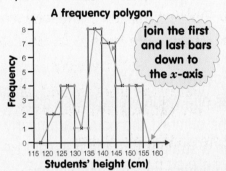

A frequency polygon

join the first and last bars down to the x-axis

Line graphs

A **line graph** is a set of points joined by a line. Line graphs can be used to show continuous data.

Example

Year	1989	1990	1991	1992	1993	1994	1995	1996
Number of cars sold	420	530	480	560	590	620	490	440

The **middle values** (for example point Y) have no meaning. Point Y does not mean that halfway between 1994 and 1995, 550 cars were sold.

 This can also be referred to as a time series since time is represented on the horizontal axis.

QUICK TEST

1. A manufacturer of chocolate asked 1440 students which type of chocolate they preferred. The pie chart shows the results. How many people preferred:

   a white chocolate
   b fruit and nut
   c milk chocolate?

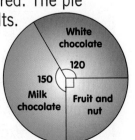

Scatter diagrams

- A *scatter diagram* (*scattergraph*) is used to show two sets of data at the same time.
- It is used to show the connection (correlation) between two sets of data.

Types of correlation

There are three types of correlation:

In the KS3 SATS you must be able to describe the types of correlation.

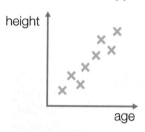

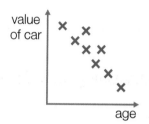

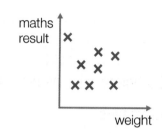

Positive correlation
As one value increases so does the other. If the points are nearly on a straight line there is said to be a **high positive correlation**.

Negative correlation
As one value increases the other decreases. If the points are nearly on a straight line there is said to be a **high negative correlation**.

Zero correlation
There is no correlation between the values.

Drawing scatter diagrams

- Work out the scales first before starting. Plot the points carefully, ticking off each point in the table as it is plotted.

Example The table shows the age of several cars and how much they are now worth.

Age (years)	1	8	4	7	6	3	5	7	3	5	2
Price (£)	5200	1200	3400	1800	2800	4000	1800	2400	4400	3000	5000

Plot the points carefully as it is easy to make mistakes.

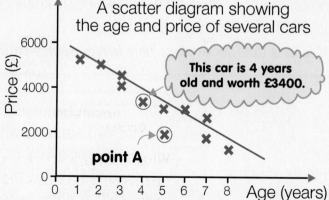

A scatter diagram showing the age and price of several cars

This car is 4 years old and worth £3400.

point A

Do not rush when drawing a scatter diagram. Plot the points very carefully.

You need to be able to interpret the scatter diagram.

- The scatter diagram shows that the older the cars become the less they are worth, i.e. there is a negative correlation.
- **Point A** shows a car which is five years old and worth £1800. This is slightly less than expected and may be due to rust or a dent, or the make.

Line of best fit

- The **line of best fit** is the line which 'best fits' the data. It goes in the direction of the data and has roughly the same number of points above it as below it.
- A line of 'best fit' can be used to make predictions.

Example

Sandra wishes to sell her car. If it is 3 years old, roughly how much would she expect to receive?

- Go across to 3 years on the horizontal axis on the diagram (on page 80). Read up to the line of best fit and then read across. Approximately £4100.

Misleading graphs

Statistical graphs are sometimes misleading; they do not tell the true story.

Examples

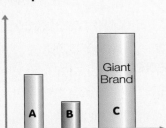

This graph is misleading because it has no scales and the bars are not the same width.

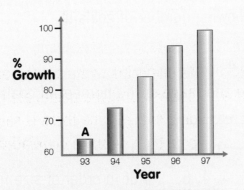

This graph is misleading because the scales do not start at zero, so the growth looks much bigger than it actually is.

This **pictogram** is misleading because the boxes change so much in volume. Although Brand B has only sold twice the amount of Brand A it gives the impression of having sold much more.

 In the exam make any criticisms clear.

KEY TERMS

Make sure you understand these terms before moving on!
- line of best fit
- negative correlation
- positive correlation
- pictogram
- scatter diagram
- scattergraph
- zero correlation

QUICK TEST

1 Look at the two graphs.

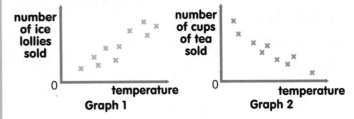

a What does Graph 1 tell you about the relationship between the number of ice lollies sold and the temperature?

b What does Graph 2 tell you about the relationship between the number of cups of tea sold and the temperature?

Averages 1

Averages of discrete data

There are three types of average: mean, median and mode.

Mean – sometimes known as the 'average'. $\text{Mean} = \dfrac{\text{sum of a set of values}}{\text{the number of values used}}$

Median – the middle value when the numbers are put in order of size.
Mode – the value that occurs the most often.
Range – tells you how much the information is spread.
Range = highest value – lowest value

Example 1

A football team scored the following number of goals in their first ten matches.

2, 4, 0, 1, 2, 2, 3, 6, 2, 4

Find the mean, median, mode and range of the number of goals scored.

Mean $= \dfrac{2 + 4 + 0 + 1 + 2 + 2 + 3 + 6 + 2 + 4}{10}$

$= \dfrac{26}{10} = 2.6$ goals ⟵ Do not round.

Median: 0, 1, 2, 2, 2, 2, 3, 4, 4, 6   Put in order of size first.

0̶ 1̶ 2̶ 2̶ (2 2) 3̶ 4̶ 4̶ 6̶   Cross off from the ends to find the middle.

Median $= \dfrac{2 + 2}{2} = 2$ goals

If there are two numbers in the middle, the median is halfway between them.

Mode = 2 goals, because it occurs four times
Range = 6 – 0 = 6

Remember to subtract the lowest value from the highest value to find the range.

Example 2

The mean of four numbers is 20, the mean of six other numbers is 36. What is the mean of all 10 numbers?

The sum of the four numbers is 80. $\left(\dfrac{80}{4} = 20\right)$

The sum of the six numbers is 216. $\left(\dfrac{216}{6} = 36\right)$

Mean of all 10 numbers is 29.6. $\left(\dfrac{\text{total sum}}{10} = \dfrac{80 + 216}{10} = \dfrac{296}{10} = 29.6\right)$

Example 3

The mean of four numbers is 7. Three of the numbers are 10, 4 and 8.
Find the value of the other number.

The sum of the four numbers is 28. $\left(\dfrac{28}{4} = 7\right)$

If x is the missing number: $10 + 4 + 8 + x = 28$

$22 + x = 28$

$x = 6$ The other number is 6.

Using appropriate averages

- The mean is useful when a typical value is wanted. Do not use the mean if there are extreme values, e.g. for the data 1, 2, 3, 4, 57 the value of 57 would raise the mean.
- The median is a useful average to use if there are extreme values.
- The mode is useful when the most common value is needed.

Finding averages from a frequency table

A **frequency table** shows how many of a data category occur.

Example Charlotte made this frequency table for the number of minutes late students were to registration.

Number of minutes late (x)	0	1	2	3	4
Frequency (f)	10	4	6	3	2

Two students were four minutes late.

This means that four students were one minute late for registration.

Mean

$$\text{Mean} = \frac{\text{total of the results when multiplied}}{\text{total of the frequency}}$$

$$= \frac{(10 \times 0) + (4 \times 1) + (6 \times 2) + (3 \times 3) + (2 \times 4)}{(10 + 4 + 6 + 3 + 2)}$$

Remember to find the total frequency.

$$= \frac{0 + 4 + 12 + 9 + 8}{25} = \frac{33}{25} = 1.32 \text{ minutes late}$$

💡 *When finding the mean for data in a frequency table, remember to divide by the sum of the frequencies and not by the number of groups.*

Median

There are 25 students in the class, the middle person is the 13th. From the frequency table: median number of minutes late is 1.

Number of minutes late (x)	0	1	2	3	4
Frequency (f)	10	4	6	3	2

The first 10 students

The 13th student is in here.

Mode (Modal value)

This is the value that has the highest frequency.

Mode = 0 minutes late because its frequency is higher than any others.

Range = 4 − 0 = 4 minutes.

Remember to write down the answer zero, not the number 10 (this is the frequency).

Make sure you understand these terms before moving on!
- mean
- median
- mode
- range
- frequency table

QUICK TEST

① The table shows the numbers of sisters that the students in class 9M have.

Number of sisters	0	1	2	3	4	5	6
Frequency		7	9	4	4	2	2	1

a Calculate the mean number of sisters that the students have. **C**

b What is the modal number of sisters?

Averages 2

Averages of grouped data

Mean

- When data is grouped, you cannot find exact data values.
- Estimate by using **midpoints** of the **class intervals**.
- The midpoint is the halfway value.

Example

The table shows the weights of year 9 pupils.

Weight (w kg)	Frequency (f)	Midpoint (x)	fx
40 ≤ W < 45	7	42.5	297.5
45 ≤ W < 50	4	47.5	190
50 ≤ W < 55	3	52.5	157.5
55 ≤ W < 60	1	57.5	57.5

- This is the same as before but now the frequency is multiplied by the midpoint.

Mean

$$= \frac{\sum fx}{\sum f} = \frac{(7 \times 42.5) + (4 \times 47.5) + (3 \times 52.5) + (1 \times 57.5)}{7 + 4 + 3 + 1}$$

$\sum$ just means 'sum of'.

$$= \frac{702.5}{15} = 46.8 \text{ kg (1 dp)}$$

Mode

When using **grouped data** you can only find the **modal class**.
This is the class with the highest frequency.

     Modal class = 40 ≤ W < 45

Median

For grouped data you can only find the class interval containing the median.
There are 15 pupils in the survey above, the middle person is the 8th one.
The 8th person is in the second interval.

     $45 ≤ W < 50$

If there is a question about grouped data on the SATS paper remember to work with the midpoints and divide by the total of the frequencies, not by the number of class intervals.

Finding the mean from a grouped frequency diagram

You may be asked to estimate the mean from a bar chart showing **grouped frequencies**.

Example

This bar chart shows some students' heights. Estimate the mean height.

- Firstly, work out the midpoint and frequency for each bar.
- $\sum fx = (122.5 \times 2) + (127.5 \times 4) + (132.5 \times 1) + (137.5 \times 8) + (142.5 \times 7) + (147.5 \times 4) + (152.5 \times 4) = 4185$

$$\frac{\sum fx}{\sum f} = \frac{4185}{30}$$ The mean height is 139.5 cm.

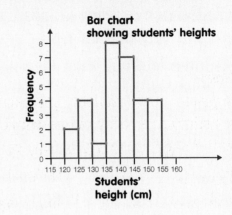

Bar chart showing students' heights

Comparing sets of data

The **ranges** and **averages** are used to compare sets of data.

Example

Class 9A obtained a mean of 57% in a science test.
Class 9T obtained a mean of 84% in the same test.

From the averages you might say 9T is better than 9A at science.
However if you look at the range for each class:

range for 9A = 100% − 21% = 79%
range for 9T = 94% − 76% = 18%

💡 *Use the range when comparing data.*

Using the range, you can see that not all pupils in 9T are better at science than those in 9A, because some 9A pupils obtained higher marks than some in 9T. The average for 9A has been lowered because of the low marks obtained by some pupils.

KEY TERMS

Make sure you understand these terms before moving on!

- average
- class interval
- grouped data
- grouped frequencies
- mean
- median
- midpoint
- modal class
- mode
- range

QUICK TEST

1. The length of the roots of some plants are recorded in the table below.

Length (L cm)	Frequency (f)
$0 \leqslant L < 5$	7
$5 \leqslant L < 10$	9
$10 \leqslant L < 15$	4
$15 \leqslant L < 20$	2

a Find an estimate for the mean length.

b What is the modal class?

Cumulative frequency

Cumulative frequency graphs (Level 8) can be used to find the median and the spread of grouped data.

■ A large interquartile range indicates that much of the data is widely spread about the median.

■ A small interquartile range indicates that much of the data is concentrated about the median.

Cumulative frequency

Ahmed carried out a survey for his Geography coursework. He recorded the distances that 200 people travelled to an out-of-town shopping centre. The table shows his findings.

Distance (d miles)	Frequency
$0 \leqslant d < 5$	12
$5 \leqslant d < 10$	49
$10 \leqslant d < 15$	57
$15 \leqslant d < 20$	45
$20 \leqslant d < 25$	34
$25 \leqslant d < 30$	3

Distance (d miles)	Cumulative frequency
$0 \leqslant d < 5$	12
$0 \leqslant d < 10$	61
$0 \leqslant d < 15$	118
$0 \leqslant d < 20$	163
$0 \leqslant d < 25$	197
$0 \leqslant d < 30$	200

■ The **cumulative frequency** is a running total, formed by adding the frequencies, e.g. 12 + 49 = 61, 61 + 57 = 118.

■ If the cumulative frequency table is correct, the final value in the cumulative frequency column should match the number of people in the survey.

■ Plot (5, 12), (10, 61), ... The upper **class boundaries** are used.

■ Since no people travelled a negative distance, the graph starts at (0, 0).

■ Join the points with a smooth curve.

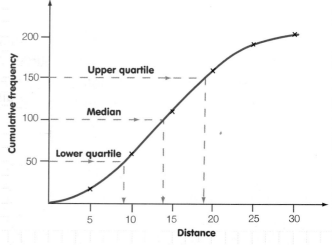

■ Cumulative frequency graphs are one of the most common topics tested on the 6–8 SATS examination. Remember to: draw graphs as accurately as possible, checking that your graph has an S-shape and try to avoid bumpy curves. Plot the upper class boundaries. Show the method lines for the median and other values on your graph.

Finding the median

The **median** is the middle value of the distribution.
For the distance data:

median = $\frac{1}{2}$ × total cumulative frequency = $\frac{1}{2}$ × 200 = 100

Reading across from 100 to the graph and then down gives a median distance of about 13.4 miles.

Finding the interquartile range

The interquartile range is found by subtracting the lower quartile from the upper quartile.
- **Interquartile range** = upper quartile – lower quartile
- **Upper quartile** is the value three-quarters of the way into the distribution.

  So $\frac{3}{4}$ × 200 = 150   Which gives an approximate value of 18.7 miles for Ahmed's data.

- **Lower quartile** This is the value one-quarter of the way into the distribution.

  So $\frac{1}{4}$ × 200 = 50   Which gives an approximate value of 9 miles for Ahmed's data.

The interquartile range for Ahmed's data is 18.7 – 9 = 9.7 miles.

QUICK TEST

On another day Bethany also carried out the same survey as Ahmed. Her results are as follows.

Distance (d miles)	Frequency
$0 \leqslant d < 5$	15
$5 \leqslant d < 10$	60
$10 \leqslant d < 15$	67
$15 \leqslant d < 20$	30
$20 \leqslant d < 25$	22
$25 \leqslant d < 30$	6

1. Draw Bethany's cumulative frequency graph on the same grid as Ahmed's.

2. Work out:

   a the median

   b the interquartile range for Bethany's data.

KEY TERMS

Make sure you understand these terms before moving on!
- class boundary
- cumulative frequency
- interquartile range
- lower quartile
- median
- upper quartile

Probability 1

What is probability?

- This is the chance that something will happen.
- **Probabilities** must be written as a **fraction**, **decimal** or **percentage**. Never use the words 'out of'.
- Probabilities can be shown on a **probability scale**. All probabilities lie from 0 to 1. No **event** has a probability less than 0 or greater than 1.

unlikely to happen

very likely to happen

0   0.5   1

definitely will not happen, e.g. I have 5 legs

evens chance, e.g. obtaining a head on a fair coin.

definitely will happen, e.g. the sun will set today

Exhaustive events account for all possible **outcomes**, for example the list 1, 2, 3, 4, 5, 6 gives all possible outcomes when a fair die is thrown.

Probability of an event not happening

If two events cannot happen at the same time:

    P(event will not happen) =
    1 – P(event will happen)

To find the probability that an event will not happen:

- Find the probability the event will happen.
- Subtract it from 1.

 To check quickly, add both numbers up and make sure you get 1.

Example

The probability that it rains today is $\frac{7}{11}$.
What is the probability that it will not rain?
    P(not rain) = 1 – P(will rain)
    P(not rain) = $1 - \frac{7}{11} = \frac{4}{11}$

Example

The probability that a torch works is
0.53. What is the probability that it does not work?
    P(does not work) = 1 – P(works)
    P(does not work) = 1 – 0.53 = 0.47

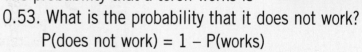

Expected number

- Probability can be used to estimate the expected number of times an event is likely to occur.

Example

The probability that Ellie obtains full marks in a spelling test is 0.4. If she takes 30 spelling tests in a year, in how many tests would you expect her to make no mistakes?
0.4 × 30 = 12 tests

Probability in practice

- Estimates of probability can be carried out by experiment or surveys.

Example 1
Based on the results of a survey we could estimate the probability that the next car to pass the school is silver.

Calculating probabilities
- Some probabilities can be calculated using the fact that each outcome is equally likely.

Probability of an event = $\dfrac{\text{number of ways an event can happen}}{\text{total number of outcomes}}$

P(event) is the shortened way of writing the probability of an event.

Example 2
There are 12 socks in a drawer: three are red, four are pink and blue and the rest are black. Nigel picks out a sock at random. What is the probability that the sock he has pulled out is:

a pink and blue **b** red **c** black **d** pink and blue, red or black **e** green?

a P(pink and blue) = $\dfrac{4}{12} = \dfrac{1}{3}$

b P(red) = $\dfrac{3}{12} = \dfrac{1}{4}$

c P(black) = $\dfrac{5}{12}$

d P(pink and blue, red or black) = $\dfrac{12}{12} = 1$

e P(green) = 0

Make sure that the number on the bottom is the total number of outcomes.

All probabilities add up to 1, so choosing a pink and blue, red or black sock will definitely happen.

There are no green socks in the drawer so the event will definitely not happen.

Whenever you answer a question on probability, check that your answer is not greater than 1. If it is you've done it wrong, so go back and try again.

QUICK TEST

1. A bag has three red, four green and ten yellow beads in it. If Reece takes out a bead at random, what is the probability that it is:
   a a red bead   b a green bead
   c a red or green bead   d a pink bead
   e a red, green or yellow bead?

2. The probability that somebody leaves a message on an answering machine is 0.32. What is the probability that they will not leave a message?

3. The probability that you pass a driving test on the first attempt is 0.35. If 200 people are taking their driving test, how many would you expect to pass first time?

Probability 2

Possible outcomes for two or more events

- It is helpful to use lists, diagrams and tables when considering outcomes of two events.

Example (Sample space diagram)

The spinner and the die are thrown together and their scores are added.

Represent the outcomes on a **sample space diagram**.

- There are 18 outcomes.

a $P(\text{score of } 6) = \frac{3}{18} = \frac{1}{6}$

b $P(\text{multiple of } 4) = \frac{5}{18}$

Spinner

2	3	④	5	6	7	⑧
2	3	④	5	6	7	⑧
1	2	3	④	5	6	7
	1	2	3	4	5	6

Die

2 on the spinner, 6 on the die, 2 + 6 = 8

It may help to put rings or squares around the numbers you need.

Example (Two-way table)

The diagram shows a **two-way table** for pupils in a class who are studying either French or German.

a If a pupil is chosen at random, what is the **probability** that they are studying French?

$$P(\text{French}) = \frac{24}{34} = \frac{12}{17}$$

Language	Male	Female	Total
French	7	17	24
German	4	6	10
Total	11	23	34

b If a girl is chosen at random, what is the probability that she is studying German?

$$P(\text{German}) = \frac{6}{23}$$ ← 6 girls study German
← 23 girls in total

Example (Tree diagram) (Level 8)

In a **tree diagram**, probabilities are written on the branches. Probabilities along each branch are multiplied to obtain the final probabilities.

The probability that Carlos is late for registration is 0.3. Find the probability that Carlos is late:

a on only one day   b on both days.

a Probability that Carlos is late on only one of the days is 0.21 + 0.21 = 0.42

b Probability that Carlos is late on both days is 0.3 × 0.3 = 0.09

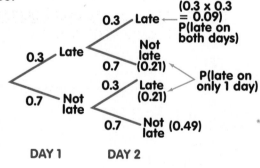

Warning! ■ You **multiply** along the branches.

■ You **add** in order to combine alternative endpoints.

> Be careful when there are two events. Use one of the ways on this page to show the information – this should make calculating probabilities easier.
> When answering questions that involve tree diagrams remember to make sure that on each pair of branches the probabilities add up to 1; multiply along the branches and add the probabilities when there is more than one alternative, i.e. P(A or B).

The multiplication law

- When two events are **independent** the outcome of the second event is not affected by the outcome of the first.
- If two or more events are independent, the probability of A and B and C ... happening together is found by multiplying the separate probabilities.

P(A and B and C ...) = P(A) × P(B) × P(C) ...

Example

The probability that it will rain on any day in August is $\frac{3}{10}$. Find the probability that:

a it will rain on both 1 August and 3 August.

P (rain and rain) = $\frac{3}{10}$ × $\frac{3}{10}$ = $\frac{9}{100}$

b it will rain on 9 August but not 20 August.

P (rain and not rain) = $\frac{3}{10}$ × $\frac{7}{10}$ = $\frac{21}{100}$

The addition law

If two or more events are **mutually exclusive** the probability of A or B or C ... happening is found by **adding** the probabilities.

P (A or B or C ...)
  = P(A) + P(B) + P(C) + ...

Example

There are 11 counters in a bag. Five of the counters are red and three of them are white. Lucy picks a counter at random. Find the probability that Lucy's counter is either red or white.

P(red) = $\frac{5}{11}$ P(white) = $\frac{3}{11}$

P(red or white) = P(red) + P(white)

$\frac{5}{11}$ + $\frac{3}{11}$ = $\frac{8}{11}$

Red and white are mutually exclusive.

Relative frequencies

- If a **fair** die is thrown 180 times, about 30 twos would be obtained. When experiments are used to estimate probabilities it is known as the **relative frequency** that the event will happen.

Relative frequency of an event
= $\dfrac{\text{number of times the event occurred}}{\text{total number of trials}}$

- As the number of throws increases, the relative frequency gets closer to the expected probability.

Example

A fair coin was thrown 80 times a head came up 35 times. What is the relative frequency of getting a head?

No. of heads = 35   No. of trials = 80

Relative frequency = $\frac{35}{80}$ = 0.4375

The theoretical probability = $\frac{1}{2}$ = 0.5

Make sure you understand these terms before moving on!

- fair
- independent
- mutually exclusive
- probability
- relative frequency
- sample space diagram
- tree diagram
- two-way table

QUICK TEST

1. A fair die is thrown 600 times. If a 5 comes up 88 times what is the relative frequency of throwing a 5?

2. Two fair dice are thrown together and their totals multiplied. Complete the sample space diagram.

   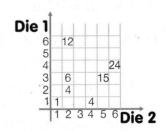

   a What is the probability of a total of 12?

   a What is the probability that the total is a multiple of 4?

Practice questions

Use the questions to test your progress. Check your answers on page 95.

1. A manufacturer of chocolate asked 200 students which type of chocolate they preferred. The pie chart shows the results. Write down how many people preferred: **C**

    a white chocolate ....

    b fruit and nut ....

    c milk chocolate ....

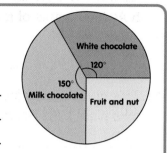

2. The letters M A T H E M A T I C S are placed on separate pieces of card and these are put into a bag. Reece picks out a card at random. Write down the probability that he picks:

    a a letter T ....   **b** a letter M ....

    c the letters A or C ....

3. Find the mean, median, mode and range of this data: **C**

    2, 4, 1, 1, 2, 3, 7, 5, 5, 5, 2, 5, 6

    ....

4. The table shows the numbers of sisters that pupils in 9G had. Calculate the mean number of sisters. Give your answer to 2 dp. **C**

Sisters (x)	0	1	2	3	4
Frequency (y)	5	15	9	2	1

5. The probability that I receive a letter is 32%. What is the probability that I will not receive a letter? ....

6. **a** Describe the correlation of the scatter diagram.

    b Draw on the graph the line of best fit.

7. The probability of passing a driving test is 0.7. If 200 people take the test today, how many would you expect to pass?

    ....

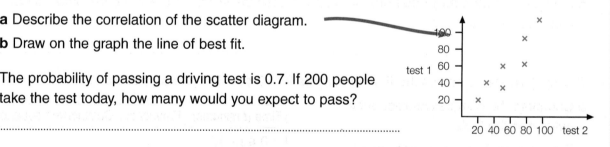

8. The diagram shows a two-way table for pupils in a class, who are studying either Italian or Spanish.

    a What is the probability that a person chosen at random studies Spanish? ....

    b What is the probability that a girl chosen at random studies Italian? ....

	Male	Female	Total
Italian	5	10	15
Spanish	12	4	16
Total	17	14	31

9. The lengths of the roots of some plants are recorded in the table: **C**

    a Find an estimate for the mean length.

    ....

    b What is the modal class?

    ....

Length (cm)	Frequency
$0 \leqslant L < 5$	6
$5 \leqslant L < 10$	9
$10 \leqslant L < 15$	15
$15 \leqslant L < 20$	9
$20 \leqslant L < 25$	6
$25 \leqslant L < 30$	2

10. A fair spinner is labelled as shown. The results of the first 12 spins are:

    A B B C A D C C A D B A

    a Write down the relative frequency of the letter A for these results.

    ....

    b As the number of results increases, what do you expect to happen to the relative frequency of
    the letter A?

    ....

11. This question was included in a survey. 'Do you agree that swimming lessons should only
    take place on a Saturday morning?' What is wrong with the question?

    ....

12. The probability that a bus is late is 0.4. By drawing a tree diagram or otherwise, calculate the
    probability that the bus is late on two consecutive days.

    ....

13. (Level 8) Ahmed and Matthew are
    going to take a swimming test.
    The probability that Ahmed will
    pass the swimming test is 0.85. The
    probability that Matthew will pass
    the swimming test is 0.6. The two
    events are independent.

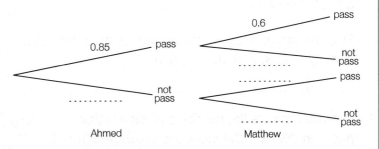

    a Complete the probability tree diagram.

    b Work out the probability that both Ahmed and Matthew will pass the swimming test.

    ....

    c Work out the probability that one of them will pass the swimming test and the other will not
    pass the swimming test.

    ....

14. (Level 8) The table shows the time in minutes for 83 people's journeys to work.

    a Complete the cumulative frequency
    column in the table.

    b Draw a cumulative frequency graph
    of the data.

    c From your graph find the median.

    d From your graph find the interquartile
    range.

    e How many people had a journey of more
    than 45 minutes to work?

Time (t minutes)	Frequency	Cumulative frequency
$0 \leqslant t < 10$	5	
$10 \leqslant t < 20$	20	
$20 \leqslant t < 30$	26	
$30 \leqslant t < 40$	18	
$40 \leqslant t < 50$	10	
$50 \leqslant t < 60$	4	

How well did you do?   ✗   1–4 Try again   5–8 Getting there   9–12 Good work   13–14 Excellent! ✓

Answers

Quick test answers

Page 5 Numbers
1. a) 3, 6, 9, 12   b) 2, 3, 5, 7, 11
   c) 1, 2, 4, 5, 10   d) 2, 4, 6, 8, 10, 12
   e) 5, 10
2. a) 10   b) 64   c) 8   d) 8
3. HCF = 5   LCM = 100

Page 7 Positive and negative numbers
1. 7°C
2. a) A = 15   b) B = 4   c) C = 4
   d) D = –10   e) E = –10   f) F = –20

Page 9 Working with numbers
1. a) 705   b) 491   c) 2208   d) 255
2. 13 113   3. 25
4. a) 152   b) 630   c) 21 000   d) 0.252
5. £12.24   6. 13

Page 11 Fractions
1. a) $x = 24$ b) $y = 25$ c) $z = 152$
2. a) $\frac{1}{3}$ b) $\frac{7}{20}$ c) $\frac{6}{13}$ d) $1\frac{1}{3}$
3. 15 pupils

Page 13 Decimals
1. a) 170.97   b) 3.84   c) 83.4   d) 15.7
2. a) 1800   b) 180   c) 18   d) 30   e) 300
   f) 50 000
3. a) 0.03, 0.037, 0.62, 0.84
   b) 22.507, 22.53, 27.06, 27.064
4. a) 12.74   b) 9.26   c) 4.17

Page 15 Percentages 1
1. 3   2. 35   3. 40
4. 22.6%   5. 82%   6. £51
7. 36 people

Page 17 Percentages 2
1. £86 515
2. a) 37.5%   b) 28.9%   c) 11.1%
3. £85.07   4. £411.76

Page 18 Equivalents
1.

Fraction	Decimal	Percentage
$\frac{3}{4}$	0.75	75%
$\frac{2}{5}$	0.4	40%
$\frac{1}{3}$	$0.\dot{3}$	$33.\dot{3}$%
$\frac{3}{5}$	0.6	60%
$\frac{1}{5}$	0.2	20%

2. 0.25, $\frac{5}{9}$, $\frac{2}{3}$, 84%, $\frac{9}{10}$

Page 19 Using a calculator
1. a) 11.73 (2 dp)   b) 0.026 (3 dp)
   c) 14.45 (2 dp)   d) 769.6 (1 dp)
2. 1.52×10^6

Page 21 Checking calculations
1. a) 0.003 79   b) 27 500   c) 307 000
2. 100   3. 10 rolls of wallpaper   4. £4.75

Page 23 Ratio
1. a) 4 : 5   b) 1 : 2   c) 5 : 2   2. £200, £300
3. 750 g   4. £2.76   5. Small tin of tuna.

Page 25 Indices
1. a) 12^{12} b) 9^{-6} c) 1   d) 18^8 e) 4^{10} f) 1
2. a) x^{13} b) $6x^{13}$ c) $4x^2$ d) $5x^{11}$ e) $2x^{12}$

Page 27 Standard index form
1. a) 6.3×10^5 b) 2.73×10^3 c) 4.29×10^{-5}
   d) 6.3×10^{-7}
2. a) 6×10^{12} b) 1.22×10^9 c) 4×10^3
   d) 3×10^{18}
3. a) 4.35×10^{10} b) 4.59×10^{16}
4. 9.76×10^{10}

Pages 28–9 Answers to practice questions
1. 20°C
2. a) 4, 8, 12   b) 2, 3, 5, 7, 11
   c) 1, 2, 3, 4, 6, 12

3. $2 \times 2 \times 2 \times 3 = 2^3 \times 3$
4. a) 10   b) 36   c) 6   d) 8
5. 7.2×10^{-5}
6. a) $x = 24$ b) $y = 25$ c) $z = 152$
7. 12%
8. 1404p or £14.04
9. 18 tins
10. a) –5   b) –1   c) –12   d) 7
11. £38.25
12. 600
13. 10.3 (1 dp)
14. 36 cm
15. a) $\frac{7}{10}$ b) $\frac{1}{6}$ c) $\frac{3}{16}$ d) $\frac{16}{27}$
16. a) 12.69   b) 28.76   c) 2.94
17. a) 273 000   b) 0.000 786   c) 27 100
18.

Fraction	Decimal	Percentage
$\frac{1}{4}$	0.25	25%
$\frac{5}{8}$	0.625	62.5%
$\frac{2}{3}$	$0.\dot{6}$	$66.\dot{6}$%

19. £6498.89
20. 0.274, $\frac{4}{7}$, 61%, $\frac{9}{10}$, 0.93, 94%
21. a) 0.006   b) 4   c) 50 000
22. a) 21.63 (2 dp)   b) 350 (3 s.f.)
23. $\frac{20^2 + 100}{8 \times 7} \approx \frac{400 + 100}{50} = 10$
24. £376.47
25. a) 2.67×10^6 b) 4.27×10^3
    c) 3.296×10^{-2} d) 2.7×10^{-2}
26. a) 1.2×10^{22} b) 2×10^{11}

Page 31 Algebra 1
1. $S = 3P + 1$ 2. a) $n + 6$ b) $p - 4$
   c) $3y + 6$ d) $\frac{h}{7}$ e) $\frac{n}{p} - 5$

Page 33 Algebra 2
1. $4a + 8$ i.e. Card C
2. a) 13.2   b) –26   c) –25.2
3. a) $2x - 6$ b) $x^2 - x - 2$ c) $x^2 - 5x + 4$
4. a) $5(x - 5)$ b) $4(3x - 5)$ c) $4(y + 4)$
5. a) $\frac{y+2}{5} = x$ b) $\frac{7y-4}{3} = x$ c) $3(y - 2) = x$
6. a) $(n + 1)(n + 1)$ b) $(n - 2)(n - 3)$
   c) $(n + 5)(n - 5)$

Page 35 Equations 1
1. $x = 5$ 2. $x = 6$ 3. $x = \frac{7}{4}$ 4. $x = 2$
5. $x = 4$ 6. $x = -1$ 7. $x = -1.4$

Page 37 Equations 2
1. a) $x = -4.5$ $y = 4$ b) $a = 2$ $b = 1$
2. a) $12x + 2 = 74$
   b) $x = 6$ ∴ length = 34 width = 3

Page 39 Inequalities
1. 4.6
2. a) $x < 6$ b) $x \geq 4$ c) $1 \leq x \leq 3$
   d) $-\frac{1}{5} \leq x < 2$

Page 41 Patterns & sequences
1. a) $4n - 1$ b) $3n + 5$ c) $n^2 + 1$
2. 2, 1

Page 43 Co-ordinates & graphs
1. a), b) See figure. c) $y = 4x$ is steeper than $y = 2x$. They both pass through the origin. d) See figure.

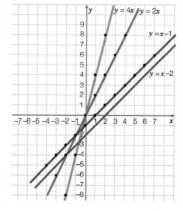

Page 45 More graphs
1.

x	–3	–2	–1	0	1	2	3
y	19	9	3	1	3	9	19

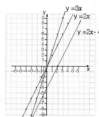

2. Graph A, $y = 3 - x^2$ Graph B, $y = \frac{2}{x}$
   Graph C, $y = 5 - x$ Graph D, $y = x^3$

Page 47 Interpreting graphs
1. Container A is graph 3, Container B is graph 1, Container C is graph 2
2. a) 20 mph   b) Staying stationary
   c) 40 mph

Pages 48–9 Answers to practice questions
1. $8a + 10b + 5$
2. a)

n	1	2	3	4	5	6
p	6	10	14	18	22	26

   b) $p = 4n + 2$
3. a) 4   b) 0   c) 17   d) 6
4. a) 320   b) 900
5. a) $4n + 8$ b) n^2 c) $2n - 2$ d) $4n + 2$
6. a) $a = 1$ b) $n = 35$
7. a), b) and d)

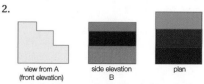

   c) $y = 3x$ is steeper than $y = 2x$, since it has a bigger gradient
8. a) $n = 3$ b) $n = -5$ c) $n = -14$
9. a) $4n + 10$ b) $4n + 10 = 22$ $n = 3$
10. $2n + 3$
11. a) $5(x + 3)$ b) $6(x - 2)$ c) $4(3x + 5)$
    d) $(n + 1)(n + 4)$ e) $(n - 2)(n - 6)$
12. a) Gradient = 4; intercept = (0, 10)
    b) Gradient = –2; intercept = (0, 6)
13. a) $66.\dot{6}$ m.p.h.   b) 1 hour   c) 50 m.p.h.
    d) 1442
14. $x = -3$, $y = 4$
15. a) $n < \frac{4}{3}$ b) $n \leq 2$
16. $n^2 + 2$
17. $x = 3(y + 6)$
18. i) D   ii) B   iii) A   iv) C

Page 51 Shapes
1. Hexagon   2. See information.

Page 53 Solids
1.

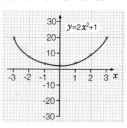

2.
view from A (front elevation)   side elevation B   plan

Page 54 Constructions & LOGO
1. Forward 2, Turn right 90°, Forward 5, Turn right 90°, Forward 2, Turn right 90°, Forward 5

2.

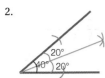

Page 55 Loci & coordinates in 3D
1.

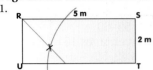

Page 57 Angles and tessellations
1. a) $a = 140°$ b) $x = 40°, y = 90°$
    c) $a = 100°, b = 80°, c = 80°$
    d) $a = 50°, b = 130°, c = 50°, d = 50°$
2. a) 60° b) 120°

Page 59 Bearings & scale drawings
1. a) 110° b) 240° c) 320°
2. a) 290° b) 060° c) 140°

Page 61 Transformations

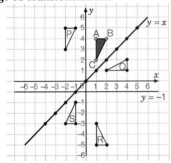

Page 63 Pythagoras' theorem
1. a) 13.8 m b) 13.3 m   2. 94.3 km

Page 65 Trigonometry
1. a) 7.5 cm b) 10.1 cm c) 18 cm
2. a) 25.6° b) 62.3° c) 36.9°
3. a) 20 cm b) 68.0 cm c) 17.1°

Page 67 Measures & measurements 1
1. 6.2 kg   2. 42 mm 3. 10.5 pints (approx)
4. A = 9.2 B = 9.5 C = 2.42 D = 2.46
    E = 2.48 F = 6.25 G = 6.75
5. $6.25 \leqslant 6.3 < 6.35$

Page 68 Measures & measurements 2
1. 4 km/h   2. 80.6 cm³
3. 45 minutes

Page 69 Similarity
1. a) 7.78 cm b) 9.12 cm

Page 71 Area & perimeter of 2D shapes
1. a) 27 cm² b) 36 cm² c) 44 cm²
    d) 19.6 cm²
2. 30.8 cm (1 dp)   3. 4 m² 4. 27 cm²

Page 73 Volume of 3D solids
1. a) 573.7 cm³ b) 96.6 cm³
    c) 1534.7 cm³
2. 48 cm³
3. a) Length b) Volume c) Volume
    d) Area

Pages 74–5 Answers to practice questions
1. i) $a = 80°$ ii) $b = 155°$
    iii) $c = 138°$ $d = 42°$
    iv) $e = 65°$ v) $f = 102°$
    vi) $g = 60°$ $h = 60°$ $i = 120°$
2. a) 6.2 kg b) 42 mm
    c) 10.5 pints (approx.)
3.

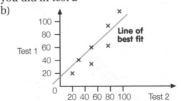

plan   elevation   elevation
         from A   from B

4. a) 15 cm² b) 17.5 cm² c) 44 cm²
5. a) 68.0 cm² b) 63.6 cm² c) 28.3 cm²
    d) 208.3 cm²
6. 30.8 cm (1 dp)

---

7. 17.6 cm² (1 dp)
8. a) 115° b) 253° c) 145°
9.

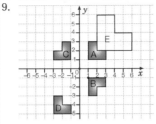

10. a) 601 cm³ (3 sf) b) 1750 cm³ (3 sf)
11. a) 16.6 m b) 10.8 m
12. 81.98 m² (2 dp)
13. 70 000 cm²
14. 56 m³
15. $9.15 \leqslant t < 9.25$
16. A = (3, 0, 0)   B = (3, 1, 0)
    C = (3, 1, 2)   D = (0, 0, 3)
    E = (1, 1, 3)   F = (1, 0, 2)
17. 9.2 m
18. a) i) XMN = 83°
        ii) XNM = XZY = 68° angles in a Δ
        add up to 180°
    b) 3.65 cm
    c) 11.7 cm
19. $v\sqrt{r^2 + t^2}$, πr^2, $2tv$

Page 77 Collecting data
1. Food type | Tally | Frequency

2. 20 | 6 9
    21 | 3 4 5
    22 | 2 7
    23 | 1 7 9
    24 | 1 3 6

Page 79 Representing information
1. a) 480 b) 360 c) 600

Page 81 Scatter diagrams
1. a) As the temperature increases, more
    ice lollies are sold (positive correlation)
    b) As the temperature increases, fewer
    cups of tea are sold (negative
    correlation)

Page 83 Averages 1
1. a) 1.83 sisters (2 dp) b) 1 sister

Page 85 Averages 2
a) 7.7 b) $5 \leqslant L < 10$

Page 87 Cumulative frequency
2. a) median approx. 12 miles
    b) interquartile range = 9 miles (approx)

Page 89 Probability 1
1. a) $\frac{3}{17}$ b) $\frac{4}{17}$ c) $\frac{7}{17}$ d) 0 e) $\frac{17}{17} = 1$
2. 0.68   3. 70

Page 91 Probability 2
1. $\frac{11}{75}$ 2. a) $\frac{4}{36} = \frac{1}{9}$ b) $\frac{15}{36} = \frac{5}{12}$

Pages 92–3 Answers to practice questions
1. a) 67 b) 50 c) 83
2. a) $\frac{2}{11}$ b) $\frac{2}{11}$ c) $\frac{3}{11}$
3. mean = 3.7 (1 dp) median = 4
    mode = 5 range = 6
4. mean = 1.34 sisters (2 dp)
5. 68% = 0.68
6. a) Positive correlation:
    the better you did in test 1 the better
    you did in test 2
    b)

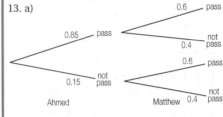

7. 140 people

---

8. a) $\frac{16}{31}$ b) $\frac{10}{14} = \frac{5}{7}$
9. a) mean = 13.1 cm (3 sf)
    b) modal class = $10 \leqslant L < 15$
10. a) $\frac{4}{12} = \frac{1}{3}$
    b) approach the expected probability
    of $\frac{1}{4}$
11. Your opinion that you only want
    swimming lessons on a Saturday
    morning is evident.
12. $0.4 \times 0.4 = 0.16$
13. a)

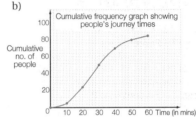

    b) 0.51
    c) 0.43
14. a)

Time (t mins)	Frequency	Cumulative frequency
$0 \leqslant t < 10$	5	5
$10 \leqslant t < 20$	20	25
$20 \leqslant t < 30$	26	51
$30 \leqslant t < 40$	18	69
$40 \leqslant t < 50$	10	79
$50 \leqslant t < 60$	4	83

    b)

Cumulative frequency graph showing people's journey times

    c) Approx. 26 min
    d) 18 min
    e) 8 people

Index